decorating
cupcakes, cakes, & cookies

decorating
cupcakes, cakes, & cookies

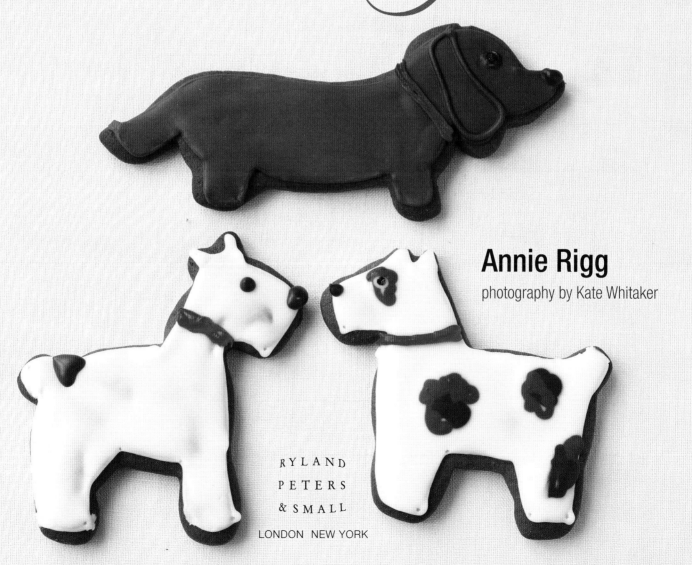

Annie Rigg

photography by Kate Whitaker

RYLAND
PETERS
& SMALL

LONDON NEW YORK

To my darling little sister, Titch.
xx

Design and photographic art direction Steve Painter
Senior editor Céline Hughes
Production controller Toby Marshall
Art director Leslie Harrington
Publishing director Alison Starling

Prop stylist Penny Markham
Indexer Hilary Bird

First published in the US in 2010 by
Ryland Peters & Small, Inc.
519 Broadway, 5th Floor
New York, NY 10012

www.rylandpeters.com

10 9 8 7 6 5 4 3 2 1

Text © Annie Rigg 2010

Design and photographs
© Ryland Peters & Small 2010

ISBN: 978-1-84597-957-7

Printed and bound in China

Library of Congress Cataloging-in-Publication Data

Rigg, Annie.
  Decorating cupcakes, cakes, & cookies / Annie Rigg ; photography by Kate Whitaker.
    p. cm.
  Includes index.
  ISBN 978-1-84597-957-7
  1. Cake decorating. 2. Cupcakes. 3. Cake. 4. Cookies. I. Title.
  TX771.2.R52 2010
  641.8'653--dc22

Notes

• All spoon measurements are level, unless otherwise specified.

• Ovens should be preheated to the specified temperature. Recipes in this book were tested using a regular oven. If using a convection oven, follow the manufacturer's instructions for adjusting temperatures.

• All eggs are large, unless otherwise specified. Recipes containing raw or partially cooked egg should not be served to the very young, very old, anyone with a compromised immune system, or pregnant women.

contents

cakes and cookies galore

For me, baking a batch of cookies or cupcakes is one of the most pleasurable ways to spend a morning. The magic of mixing together a few simple ingredients to create something so delicious, filling the kitchen with sweet, homey aromas is unrivaled. But sometimes you want to create something a little more special—something with an extra ounce or two of love.

Take a batch of cupcakes, add a luscious swirl of frosting and a little imagination, and you too can be a baking queen (or king). It's the little things that can make all the difference and elevate a simple tray of brownies or cookies to the next level.

You don't need any great skill or even to possess a huge array of fancy kitchen equipment to make something unique. Most of the recipes in this book use standard cake pans and equipment. All you need is a couple of piping bags, a selection of tips, an assortment of cookie cutters, and a rainbow of food coloring pastes. All of these are now widely available in most cookware stores or from online suppliers. And there are so many beautiful sprinkles and sparkles for the home baker to use that it seems crazy not to make the most of them.

Most of the recipes in this book can be made partially in advance, whether that be the cookie dough, the cake, or the even the embellishments. Some of the recipes come with simple and easy-to-follow steps to guide you through the decorating techniques. There's a recipe for you however wobbly your baking skills might be, starting with simple gingerbread men (and women) right up to making sugar-paste roses for decorating a wedding cake.

These cookies, cakes, and cupcakes are perfect as gifts, for that special party, or just to cheer up a friend. How fabulous would it be to give your loved one a tray of Valentine's cupcakes instead of giving them an unimaginative bunch of roses or box of chocolates?

How many times have you wished you could recreate the fabulous confections you see in cake store windows? Well, now you can. So turn the oven on, get your mixer out, go wild with the piping bag, and start a love affair with sprinkles.

the basics

basic cakes

A freestanding electric mixer makes light work of cake making, cutting down on time and energy, but you can also use an electric whisk or a good old-fashioned wooden spoon. When mixing cake batter, it is important to remember that all ingredients, including buttermilk, sour cream, and eggs, should be at room temperature.

buttermilk cake

This base can be used for both small and large cakes. Paper cupcake cases can vary enormously in size, so it's safest to suggest filling the cases two-thirds full. This recipe makes 12–16 regular cupcakes depending on the cases used. Unfrosted cupcakes can be frozen in plastic airtight boxes.

12 tablespoons unsalted butter, softened
1 cup sugar
2 whole eggs and 1 egg yolk, beaten
1 teaspoon pure vanilla extract
1¾ cups all-purpose flour
1 teaspoon baking powder
½ teaspoon baking soda
½ cup buttermilk

makes 12–16 cupcakes

Cream together the butter and sugar until light and creamy. Gradually add the beaten eggs, mixing well between each addition and scraping down the side of the mixing bowl from time to time. Add the vanilla.

Sift together the flour, baking powder, and baking soda and add to the mixture in alternate batches with the buttermilk. Mix until smooth and then turn to the relevant recipe.

double chocolate cake

This recipe is deep and densely chocolatey. It makes 12 regular cupcakes depending on the cases used, but can easily be doubled.

3 oz. bittersweet chocolate, chopped
3 tablespoons unsalted butter, softened
¾ cup packed light brown sugar
2 eggs, beaten
½ teaspoon pure vanilla extract
1 cup plus 2 tablespoons all-purpose flour
1 heaping tablespoon cocoa powder
½ teaspoon baking powder
1 teaspoon baking soda
a pinch of salt
½ cup sour cream
6 tablespoons boiling water

makes about 12 cupcakes

Melt the chocolate in a microwave or in a heatproof bowl set over a pan of barely simmering water. Cream together the butter and sugar until light and creamy. Gradually add the beaten eggs, mixing well between each addition and scraping down the side of the mixing bowl from time to time. Add the vanilla and melted chocolate and stir well. Sift the flour, cocoa, baking powder, baking soda, and salt together. Add to the mixture in alternate batches with the sour cream. Add the boiling water and mix well. Turn to the relevant recipe.

yellow butter cake

This is a very simple, delicate cake with a hint of vanilla. Feel free to swap the vanilla extract for finely grated unwaxed lemon zest and ½ teaspoon lemon extract.

12 tablespoons unsalted butter, softened
¾ cup plus 2 tablespoons sugar
3 eggs, beaten
1 teaspoon pure vanilla extract
1⅓ cups all-purpose flour
3 teaspoons baking powder
3 tablespoons milk

makes 12–16 cupcakes

Cream together the butter and sugar until light and creamy. Gradually add the beaten eggs, mixing well between each addition and scraping down the side of the mixing bowl from time to time. Add the vanilla.

Sift together the flour and baking powder and add to the mixture in 2 batches. Stir in the milk. Mix until smooth and then turn to the relevant recipe.

cookie doughs

Most of the cookie recipes in this book can be made with one of the doughs below. Remember to chill the dough for a good couple of hours before rolling out and shaping into cookies. Before frosting cookies, make sure they are completely cold after baking, or the frosting will simply melt or slide off.

basic vanilla cookies

These cookies will keep unfrosted for 3 days in an airtight box. If they've been frosted, they should be eaten within 24 hours.

15 tablespoons unsalted butter, at room temperature
1 cup plus 2 tablespoons sugar
1 egg, beaten
½ teaspoon pure vanilla extract
a pinch of salt
3½ cups all-purpose flour, sifted, plus extra for dusting

Cream together the butter and sugar until light and creamy. Add the beaten egg, vanilla, and salt and mix well.

Gradually add the flour and mix until incorporated. Bring together into a dough, then flatten into a disk. Wrap in plastic wrap and refrigerate for 2 hours.

Roll the dough out on a lightly floured work surface to a thickness of ⅛ inch and then turn to the relevant recipe.

Remember that once you have stamped out the shapes required in the individual recipes, you can gather the remaining dough together into a ball and re-roll to make more shapes. The shapes will then need to be refrigerated for a further 15 minutes before baking.

gingerbread cookies

These cookies will keep unfrosted for 3 days in an airtight box. If they've been frosted, they should be eaten within 24 hours.

a scant 3 cups all-purpose flour
½ teaspoon baking powder
1 teaspoon baking soda
1 teaspoon ground cinnamon
1 tablespoon ground ginger
¼ teaspoon ground cloves
¼ teaspoon grated nutmeg
¼ teaspoon ground allspice
a pinch of cayenne pepper
a pinch of salt
1 stick unsalted butter, softened
⅓ cup packed light brown sugar
1 egg, beaten
3 tablespoons honey
3 tablespoons molasses
1 tablespoon freshly squeezed lemon juice

Sift together the flour, baking powder, baking soda, spices, and salt.

Cream together the butter and sugar until light and creamy. Add the beaten egg, honey, molasses, and lemon juice and mix until smooth. Add the sifted dry ingredients and mix again until smooth. Knead the dough lightly, just enough to bring it together, then wrap in plastic wrap and refrigerate for 2 hours.

frostings

Everyone has their favorite frosting—mine is meringue buttercream. Whether piped into mountain-high peaks or spread with an artistic flourish, it really is the icing on the cake, so go wild with the food coloring and tint your frosting any or all the colors of the rainbow. Royal icing is perfect for frosting cookies, as it can be easily colored with food coloring pastes and piped into shapes and patterns, and it sets firm on the cookies.

marshmallow frosting

This is very simple, but you really do need a candy thermometer to check the temperature of the meringue as it cooks, otherwise it might not be a success. This frosting should be used immediately once prepared, as it will set into a firm marshmallow once cooled.

1¼ cups sugar
1 tablespoon water
4 egg whites
a pinch of salt

Put all the ingredients in a heatproof bowl set over a pan of simmering water. Whisk slowly until the sugar has dissolved and the mixture is foamy. Continue cooking until the mixture reaches at least 140°F on a candy thermometer.

Immediately pour the frosting into the bowl of a freestanding mixer fitted with the whisk attachment (or use an electric whisk and mixing bowl) and beat on medium speed for about 3 minutes until the meringue is stiff and glossy. Use immediately.

meringue buttercream

I love this frosting. It's lighter than basic buttercream because of the meringue element, but it does take a little more effort to make. As with the Marshmallow Frosting, you really do need a candy thermometer to check the temperature of the meringue as it cooks. Add the butter to the meringue only when the meringue is cooled otherwise the butter will melt and curdle the frosting.

1 cup sugar
3 egg whites
2 sticks unsalted butter, softened and chopped
1 teaspoon pure vanilla extract

Put the sugar and egg whites in a heatproof bowl set over a pan of simmering water. Whisk until it reaches at least 140°F on a candy thermometer. Pour into the bowl of a freestanding electric mixer fitted with the whisk attachment (or use an electric whisk and mixing bowl). Beat until the mixture has doubled in volume, cooled, and will stand in stiff, glossy peaks—this will take about 3 minutes.

Gradually add the butter to the cooled meringue mix, beating constantly, until the frosting is smooth. Fold in the vanilla and use immediately.

chocolate meringue buttercream

A lighter option than the Chocolate Fudge Frosting overleaf, this is perfect for piping. Any that's left over can be stored in the refrigerator in an airtight box for a couple of days, but bring to room temperature and beat until smooth before using.

9 oz. bittersweet chocolate, chopped
1 cup plus 2 tablespoons sugar
5 egg whites
a pinch of salt
1 lb. unsalted butter, softened and chopped

Melt the chocolate either in a microwave or in a heatproof bowl set over a pan of barely simmering water.

Put the sugar, egg whites, and salt in a heatproof bowl set over a pan of simmering water. Whisk until it reaches at least 140°F on a candy thermometer. Pour into the bowl of a freestanding electric mixer fitted with the whisk attachment (or use an electric whisk and mixing bowl). Beat until the meringue holds stiff, glossy peaks.

Gradually add the butter, beating between each addition. Fold in the melted chocolate, then cover until ready to use.

vanilla buttercream

This simple buttercream can be made in a variety of flavors, not just vanilla. Lemon, peppermint, or pistachio extract and rosewater can easily be substituted for the vanilla.

3 sticks unsalted butter, softened
3 cups confectioners' sugar, sifted
a few drops of pure vanilla extract (optional)

Put the butter in a large bowl and, using a freestanding mixer or electric whisk, cream until really soft. Gradually add the sifted confectioners' sugar and beat until pale and smooth. Beat in the vanilla, if using.

chocolate ganache

This is a classic topping for sophisticated cakes. Use the best-quality chocolate for this recipe.

6½ oz. bittersweet chocolate (at least 70% cocoa solids), chopped
5 tablespoons unsalted butter
2 tablespoons heavy cream

Put the chocolate, butter, and cream in a heatproof bowl set over a pan of simmering water. Stir until smooth and thoroughly combined. Set aside to cool and thicken slightly before using.

chocolate fudge frosting

This is the ultimate chocolate frosting—deep and luscious. Sweep generous swirls of it on top of vanilla or chocolate cupcakes, scatter with colored sprinkles, and you'll be the cupcake queen (or king).

11 oz. bittersweet chocolate, chopped
15 tablespoons unsalted butter
1 scant cup milk
1 teaspoon pure vanilla extract
3⅓ cups confectioners' sugar, sifted

Put the chocolate and butter in a heatproof bowl set over a pan of simmering water. Stir until smooth and thoroughly combined. Set aside to cool slightly.

In another bowl, whisk together the milk, vanilla, and confectioners' sugar until smooth. Add the cooled chocolate mixture and stir until smooth. Allow the frosting to set and thicken slightly before using.

chocolate glaze

A glossy, silky-smooth glaze for perfectly coating cakes or cookies.

9½ oz. bittersweet chocolate, chopped
2 tablespoons sunflower or peanut oil

Put the chocolate and oil in a heatproof bowl set over a pan of simmering water. Stir until smooth and thoroughly combined. Set aside to cool for about 10 minutes before using.

cream cheese frosting

Carrot cake is unthinkable without this frosting. Add more or less honey according to taste, as some cream cheeses can be more salty than others. The cherry on top? A dusting of ground cinnamon. Lovely.

1 lb. cream cheese
2–3 heaping tablespoons honey

Beat the ingredients together in a mixing bowl until smooth.

mascarpone frosting

This makes an excellent alternative to the more classic Cream Cheese Frosting above and can be used for carrot or banana cakes. It's also an excellent partner for summer berry cakes, and can be used as both a filling and topping for layer cakes. Add the seeds of half a vanilla bean to take it to the next level.

⅔ cup cream cheese
⅔ cup mascarpone
5 tablespoons unsalted butter, softened
⅔ cup confectioners' sugar, sifted

Beat all the ingredients together in a mixing bowl until smooth.

royal icing

This can easily be made using the method below, or with storebought royal icing sugar—simply follow the instructions on the package. It's perfect for piping lines, squiggles, and flourishes.

2 egg whites
4–4½ cups confectioners' sugar, sifted

Beat the egg whites until foamy using a wire whisk. Gradually add the confectioners' sugar and whisk until the desired stiffness is reached—for piping, the icing should hold a solid ribbon trail. If you're not using it immediately, cover with plastic wrap.

To make shapes, fit a piping bag with the required tip and fill with the royal icing. Line a baking sheet with baking parchment and pipe shapes onto the paper. Set aside for at least 24 hours until set solid.

Shapes will keep for up to 1 week in an airtight container. Keep the shapes between layers of waxed paper.

storebought sugar paste, regal icing, and ready-to-roll fondant

These 3 types of ready-made icings are available either in the baking aisle of some supermarkets or from sugarcraft suppliers (see page 126).

Sugar paste can be colored using food coloring paste (see page 16) and is ideal for rolling out to make shapes like flowers. It is usually used for more decorative items that need to set solid and dry quickly. See, for example, the flowers for the Rich Chocolate Celebration Cake on page 109 and Blossom Cake on page 125.

Regal icing or ready-made royal icing is slightly softer than sugar paste and can be colored or flavored using food coloring pastes and flavors. It is suitable as a cake covering and for modeling flowers.

Ready-to-roll fondant icing is more often used for cake coverings and will set softer than the royal or regal icing (see Blossom Cake on page 123).

All of these icings are widely available in either white or ivory, but can also be found in a variety of colors from specialty sugarcraft suppliers.

piping tips and bags

If you plan on making lots of decorated cakes and cookies, it is worth considering investing in a selection of piping tips in varying shapes and sizes. Piping bags also come in a variety of materials and sizes. Look out for easy-to-use disposable plastic piping bags that usually come in packs of 24 and can be trimmed either to a point or to fit most tips.

1

2

3

4

5

how to make
2 paper piping bags

✳ Cut a large piece of baking parchment into a square. Fold the square in half diagonally, then cut along the fold to give you 2 triangles.

✳ Take 1 triangle. With the longest side closest to you, take the right-hand corner and turn it inward toward the top corner to create the start of a cone. **(1)**

✳ Wrap the left-hand corner around the cone. **(2)**

✳ The left-hand corner should meet the top of the cone, underneath and facing the original, right-hand corner. Neaten the points so that you have a tight cone. **(3)**

✳ Flatten the cone—there will now be a triangle of paper sticking out of the top. Fold this over a few times to secure the bag **(4)**.

✳ Snip off the very tip. **(5)**

✳ Repeat to make another piping bag.

tinting royal icing

✳ Follow the recipe for Royal Icing on page 13. Using either a wooden skewer or toothpick, add tiny amounts of food coloring paste to the icing. **(1)**

✳ Mix thoroughly before adding more coloring. Remember that some colors can intensify over time, so always add the coloring in very small amounts. **(2)**

tinting fondant icing, sugar paste, or marzipan

✳ Using a wooden skewer or toothpick, add tiny amounts of food coloring paste to fondant icing, sugar paste, or marzipan. **(3)**

✳ Knead until smooth and add more coloring accordingly. Remember that some colors can intensify over time so always add the coloring gradually. **(4)**

food coloring pastes

These are now widely available in sugarcraft and good kitchen stores, and online from specialty cake decorating suppliers. They come in a rainbow of colors and can be used in tiny quantities without diluting your icing, making them much easier to work with than liquid colors.

embossing sugar paste and fondant icing

Embossing tools are a very effective way of creating simple, decorative patterns on either sugar paste or fondant icing. They can be bought from cake decorating and sugarcraft suppliers (see page 126). Alternatively, look around your kitchen and you may find some unlikely embossing tools: the fine side of a grater gently pressed into icing can create a delicate pattern; the underside of antique silver cutlery and the points of piping tips can also make unusual shapes and designs.

1

2

frosting cupcakes

✳ Always make sure that any cakes you are decorating are completely cold before frosting them, otherwise the frosting will simply melt and slide off the tops.

✳ There are so many ways you can top a cupcake that there really are no rules. It's completely up to you! For simplicity, you can spread the frosting onto the top of the cakes in generous swirls using a palette knife. **(1)**

✳ If you prefer, you can pipe the frosting into more structured shapes. Fit a large piping bag with your chosen tip, fill the bag with frosting, twist the top of the bag so that the frosting is pushed to the end toward the tip, and away you go! If you're not happy with your piping results, simple scoop the frosting off the top of the cake and start again.

✳ Remember that you can use different-shaped tips to create a variety of effects with frosting (see page 14). The Signature Cupcakes on page 92 were achieved with a star tip. When you've practiced your piping technique and gained in confidence, try the Little Flower Pots on page 94—they're bound to impress!

✳ There are hundreds of sprinkles to choose from for scattering over your frosted cupcake. For the simplest retro decoration, cover the top of some cupcakes with frosting, spreading it right to the edges, tip your chosen sprinkles onto a plate or into a shallow bowl, and simply roll the edges of the cakes into the sprinkles. **(2)**

other quick decorating ideas

✳ Look for stencils at cake decorating or sugarcraft suppliers. Made of plastic, they are available in a variety of designs and sizes. Dust either confectioners' sugar, cocoa powder, or edible colored powders directly onto cookies or cakes.

✳ If you have patience and a steady hand, you could use a fine, soft brush to paint lusters directly onto fondant-covered cakes.

✳ Paper doilies make brilliant cheap and pretty stencils, and come in a variety of sizes and patterns. Alternatively, you could get creative with some paper and scissors and make your own stencil designs.

sprinkles

There is a huge variety of decorating sprinkles available to the home cook. They range from simple and classic jimmies, to pastel-colored butterflies, Valentine's hearts, and miniature chocolate drops and candies. Look out for seasonal shapes at cake decorating or sugarcraft suppliers.

glitters, sparkles, and luster dust

Use glitters, sparkles, and luster dust to add wow factor to your decorations. These are widely available at cake decorating or sugarcraft suppliers (see page 126). They come in all the colors of the rainbow and can simply be sprinkled or painted over decorations. Although edible, they should be used sparingly.

cookies

Now there's a funny thing: a cookie that wants to be a cupcake—or is it a cupcake that wants to be a cookie? The particular cookie cutter that I have used for this recipe is a cupcake topped with a candle. To make the candle more realistic I have used gold leaf for the flame, but you could simply paint the flame using food coloring pastes.

cupcake cookies

1 quantity Basic Vanilla Cookies (page 10)

1 quantity Royal Icing (page 13)

pink food coloring paste

blue food coloring paste

pink, red, and white sprinkles

edible gold leaf or dust (optional)

cupcake-shaped cookie cutter

2 baking sheets, lined with baking parchment

small piping bag with a fine writing tip, or make your own (see page 15)

mini palette knife or small knife

makes about 18

You should have rolled out the Basic Vanilla Cookie dough to a thickness of ⅛ inch on a lightly floured work surface. Using the cupcake cookie cutter, carefully stamp out shapes. Arrange them on the prepared baking sheets. Gather together the scraps of the dough and re-roll to make more shapes. Refrigerate for 15 minutes.

Preheat the oven to 350°F.

Bake the cookies on the middle shelf of the preheated oven for about 12 minutes, or until golden, swapping the sheets around if needed. Let cool on the sheets for about 5 minutes before transferring to a wire rack to cool completely.

Divide the Royal Icing between 3 bowls. Tint one pink and one blue (see page 16 for help on tinting) using the food coloring pastes. Tint them the shade of pink or blue you like by very gradually adding more coloring. Leave the third bowl of icing white.

Fill the piping bag with whichever color you want to start with. Pipe borders around the cold cookies. "Flood" the area inside the borders with icing (see page 44 for step pictures of "flooding"): once you have made a neat border, you can spoon icing within the borders and spread it carefully up to the edges with a mini palette knife or small knife. Let it dry and harden slightly before you pipe any lines on top of the flooded icing. Decorate as you like with the sprinkles.

Attach a small piece of edible gold leaf to the flame of the candle with a little brush. Allow to set before serving.

Look for snowflake cookie cutters in sets of assorted shapes and sizes. Once covered in fondant icing, these cookies can be decorated in a vast array of nonpareils, luster dust, and glitter, which all help to create that festive, frosty feel.

snowflakes

1 quantity Gingerbread Cookies (page 10)

all-purpose flour, for dusting

confectioners' sugar, for dusting

8–10 oz. white ready-to-roll fondant icing

2 tablespoons sieved apricot jam, warmed

½ quantity Royal Icing (page 13)

silver and/or white edible glitter, luster dust, and nonpareils

snowflake cookie cutters in assorted shapes and sizes

2 baking sheets, lined with baking parchment

small piping bag with a fine writing tip, or make your own (see page 15)

embossing tools (optional)

festive string or narrow ribbon (optional)

makes 12–16

Preheat the oven to 350°F.

Take the Gingerbread Cookie dough out of the refrigerator and put it on a lightly floured work surface. Roll it out to a thickness of ⅛ inch. Using the snowflake cookie cutters, carefully stamp out shapes. Arrange them on the prepared baking sheets. Gather together the scraps of the dough and re-roll to make more shapes. If you are making these cookies to hang as Christmas decorations, using a wooden skewer, make a hole in the top of each snowflake big enough to push your ribbon through.

Bake the cookies on the middle shelf of the preheated oven for 10–12 minutes, or until firm and the edges are just starting to brown, swapping the sheets around if needed. Let cool on the sheets for about 5 minutes before transferring to a wire rack to cool completely.

Lightly dust a work surface with confectioners' sugar. Roll out the fondant icing to a thickness of no more than ⅛ inch. Using the snowflake cookie cutters again, stamp out snowflakes to match each of your cookies. Lightly brush the top of each cold cookie with the warmed apricot jam. Carefully position one fondant snowflake on top of each cookie, gently smoothing into place with your hands.

Fill the piping bag with the Royal Icing and pipe a border around the edge of the fondant icing on each cookie. Decorate with lines and dots—whatever strikes your fancy. While the royal icing is still wet, sprinkle edible glitter, luster dust, and nonpareils over it so that they stick in place.

Using embossing tools (see page 17), press decorative patterns into the fondant icing, if you like. If you have made holes in the cookies to hang them, you will need to push the skewer into the fondant to make a hole in the same place. Let the cookies dry, then push a length of string or ribbon through each hole and tie a knot to secure.

These little cookies work best when made into simple shapes such as stars and flowers. The decoration is in the colorful "stained-glass" center, so the simpler the shape of the cookie, the more eye-catching the design. These are a great idea for children's parties—kids love the pretty colors and jewel-like effect.

stained-glass cookies

1 quantity Basic Vanilla Cookies (page 10)

1 bag fruit-flavored hard candies

selection of shaped cookie cutters

2 baking sheets, lined with baking parchment

makes about 24

You should have rolled out the Basic Vanilla Cookie dough to a thickness of ⅛ inch on a lightly floured work surface. Using the cookie cutters, carefully stamp out shapes. Arrange them on the prepared baking sheets. Using smaller cutters, cut out a shape in the center of each cookie. Gather together the scraps of the dough and re-roll to make more shapes. Refrigerate for 15 minutes.

Preheat the oven to 350°F.

Divide the hard candies into separate colors and pop into plastic food bags. Using a rolling pin or mortar and pestle, crush the candies into small pieces.

Take the rolled cookies out of the refrigerator. Carefully fill the empty space in the center of each cookie with the crushed candies in an even, thin layer and no thicker than the depth of the cookies.

Bake one baking sheet at a time on the middle shelf of the preheated oven for about 12 minutes, or until the cookies are pale golden and the candy has melted to fill the space.

Let the cookies cool on the sheets until the "stained glass" has set.

Look for images of Russian dolls and use them as templates for these cookies. I found a shape I liked and just photocopied it in 3 different sizes. Simply cut out the paper template, lay it onto the rolled-out cookie dough, and cut around it using a small, sharp knife. You can also now find cookie-cutter kits to make your own shapes.

russian dolls

1 quantity Basic Vanilla Cookies or Gingerbread Cookies (page 10)

all-purpose flour, for dusting

2 quantities Royal Icing (page 13)

red food coloring paste

black food coloring paste

red, pink, and white heart- and star-shaped sugar sprinkles

russian doll-shaped paper templates

2 baking sheets, lined with baking parchment

small piping bag with a fine writing tip, or make your own (see page 15)

mini palette knife or small knife

makes about 8—10 depending on size

If you haven't already done so, roll out the Basic Vanilla Cookie or Gingerbread Cookie dough to a thickness of ⅛ inch on a lightly floured work surface. Lay your paper templates directly on top of the dough and cut around using a small, sharp knife. Arrange them on the prepared baking sheets. Gather together the scraps of the dough and re-roll to make more shapes. Refrigerate for 15 minutes.

Preheat the oven to 350°F.

Bake the cookies on the middle shelf of the preheated oven for about 12 minutes, or until firm, swapping the sheets around if needed. Let cool on the sheets for about 10 minutes before transferring to a wire rack to cool completely.

Divide the Royal Icing between 3 bowls. Tint one red and one black (see page 16 for help on tinting) using the food coloring pastes. Leave the third bowl of icing white.

Fill the piping bag with whichever color you want to start with. Pipe borders around the cold cookies. If you want to make the "belly" of the doll in the other color of icing, you will need to create a border for this too. "Flood" the area inside the borders with icing (see page 44 for step pictures of "flooding"): once you have made a neat border, you can spoon icing within the borders and spread it carefully up to the edges with a mini palette knife or small knife. Let dry and harden slightly before going any further.

Pipe in the rest of the design and the dolls' faces. Now the fun starts: you can feather the icing using a wooden skewer or toothpick (see pages 48–9 for steps on feathering) or pipe small flowers, dots, squiggles, and whatever you like over the dolls. Arrange the shaped sugar sprinkles all over. Allow to set before serving.

This recipe makes approximately 12 cookies or 6 pairs of shoes, depending on the size of your cutters. Why not decorate the cookies to match your favorite outfit or to coordinate with a special occasion such as a bachelorette party or wedding?

a girl can never have enough shoes

1 quantity Basic Vanilla Cookies or Gingerbread Cookies (page 10)

all-purpose flour, for dusting

8–10 oz. white ready-to-roll fondant icing or sugar paste

red food coloring paste

confectioners' sugar, for dusting

2 tablespoons sieved apricot jam, warmed

pearly nonpareils

edible sugar diamonds (optional)

high-heeled shoe-shaped cookie cutter

2 baking sheets, lined with baking parchment

very small, round cookie cutter

embossing tools

makes about 6 pairs

If you haven't already done so, roll out the Basic Vanilla Cookie or Gingerbread Cookie dough to a thickness of ⅛ inch on a lightly floured work surface. Using the shoe cookie cutter, carefully stamp out shapes. Arrange them on the prepared baking sheets. Gather together the scraps of the dough and re-roll to make more shapes. Refrigerate for 15 minutes.

Preheat the oven to 350°F.

Bake the cookies on the middle shelf of the preheated oven for about 12 minutes, or until firm, swapping the sheets around if needed. Let cool on the sheets for about 5 minutes before transferring to a wire rack to cool completely.

Divide the fondant icing (or sugar paste) into 2. Tint one portion red (see page 16 for help on tinting) using the food coloring paste. Tint it the shade of red you like by very gradually adding more coloring. Leave the other half white.

Lightly dust a work surface with confectioners' sugar. Roll out the 2 colors of fondant icing to a thickness of ⅟₁₆ inch. Using the shoe cookie cutter again, stamp out shoes to match each of your cookies. Using the very small, round cookie cutter, stamp out circles all over each shoe. Carefully remove the circles and reserve them.

Lightly brush the top of each cold cookie with the warmed apricot jam. Carefully position one fondant shoe on top of each cookie, gently smoothing into place with your hands. Use any scraps to make bows, ribbons, and embellishments for your shoes. Take your little red reserved circles and slot them into the holes in your white shoes. Repeat with the white circles and red shoes. Stick the embellishments onto the shoes with a tiny dab of cold water.

Using embossing tools (see page 17), decorate the shoes with patterns and gently press pearly nonpareils and/or sugar diamonds into the designs. Allow to set before serving.

Gingerbread people come in a variety of shapes, sizes, and states of undress! You could make simple gingerbread men (or women) with their more traditional decoration of currant eyes and buttons, or go for something a little more unique such as Adam and Eve, complete with fondant-icing fig leaves protecting their modesty. To make the leaves, you can either attempt to cut out the shapes freehand using a small, sharp knife, or you can make a paper template, lay it on the icing, and cut around it. The flower in Eve's hair is made like those on page 125.

gingerbread adam and eve

1 quantity Gingerbread Cookies (page 10)

all-purpose flour, for dusting

3½ oz. white ready-to-roll fondant icing

green food coloring paste

confectioners' sugar, for dusting

gingerbread man-shaped cookie cutter

2 baking sheets, lined with baking parchment

very small and medium flower-shaped cutters

makes about 8–10 depending on size

Preheat the oven to 350°F.

Take the Gingerbread Cookie dough out of the refrigerator and put it on a lightly floured work surface. Roll it out to a thickness of ⅛ inch. Using the gingerbread man cookie cutter, carefully stamp out shapes. Arrange them on the prepared baking sheets. Gather together the scraps of the dough and re-roll to make more shapes.

Bake the cookies on the middle shelf of the preheated oven for 10–12 minutes, or until firm and the edges are just starting to brown, swapping the sheets around if needed. Let cool on the sheets for about 5 minutes before transferring to a wire rack to cool completely.

If you'd like to make the white flowers as hair accessories for Eve, divide the fondant icing into 2. (If you are only making fig leaves, you don't need to divide it up.) Tint one portion green (see page 16 for help on tinting) using the food coloring paste. Tint it the shade of green you like by very gradually adding more coloring. Leave the other half white.

Lightly dust a work surface with confectioners' sugar. Roll out the 2 colors of fondant icing to a thickness of ⅟₁₆ inch. Cut out fig leaf shapes with a small, sharp knife or use a paper template. Mark out the leaf veins with a toothpick or the back of a knife. Stamp out flowers with the very small flower-shaped cookie cutter for Eve's extra covering. To make flowers for Eve's hair, use the medium flower-shaped cutter and follow the instructions on page 125.

Stick the fig leaves, bikini flowers, and hair accessories onto each cold cookie in the correct position with a little dab of cold water!

Look for sets of assorted Easter-related cookie cutters, but if you can't find them, make paper templates, lay over the cookie dough, and carefully cut out using a small, sharp knife. I've made my Easter bunnies using an extra-large cutter, but feel free to use a smaller breed!

easter eggs and bunnies

1 quantity Basic Vanilla Cookies or Gingerbread Cookies (page 10)

all-purpose flour, for dusting

2 quantities Royal Icing (page 13)

brown food coloring paste

pink food coloring paste

blue food coloring paste

lilac food coloring paste

black food coloring paste

white nonpareils or sugar strands

easter egg-shaped cookie cutters

bunny rabbit-shaped cookie cutter

2 baking sheets, lined with baking parchment

small piping bag with a fine writing tip, or make your own (see page 15)

mini palette knife or small knife

narrow checked ribbon (optional)

makes about 10—12 depending on size

If you haven't already done so, roll out the Basic Vanilla Cookie or Gingerbread Cookie dough to a thickness of ⅛ inch on a lightly floured work surface. Using the cookie cutters, carefully stamp out egg and bunny shapes. Arrange them on the prepared baking sheets. Gather together the scraps of the dough and re-roll to make more shapes. Refrigerate for 15 minutes.

Preheat the oven to 350°F.

Bake the cookies on the middle shelf of the preheated oven for about 12 minutes, or until firm, swapping the sheets around if needed. Let cool on the sheets for about 5 minutes before transferring to a wire rack to cool completely.

Divide the Royal Icing between 6 bowls. Tint each one a different color (see page 16 for help on tinting) using the food coloring pastes. You will only need a tiny amount of the black icing. Leave the last bowl of icing white.

Fill the piping bag with whichever color you want to start with. Pipe borders around the cold egg-shaped cookies. "Flood" the area inside the borders with icing (see page 44 for step pictures of "flooding"): once you have made a neat border, you can spoon icing within the borders and spread it carefully up to the edges with a mini palette knife or small knife. Let dry and harden slightly before going any further.

Pipe in the rest of the design: draw lines, squiggles, and dots over each egg. Set aside to dry completely.

Repeat the same technique for icing the bunnies using brown icing. Pipe in noses, mouths, and eyes with the black icing. Finish off each rabbit with a fluffy tail: pipe a large blob of white icing in the correct position and scatter with the nonpareils or sugar strands.

Once the icing has completely set, tie a length of checked ribbon around the neck of each bunny and serve alongside the eggs.

These cookies are like a ray of sunshine on a gray day. Any type of flower-shaped cookie cutter can be used. Why not use a variety of shapes and sizes to make a flower cookie bouquet?

sunflowers

1 quantity Basic Vanilla Cookies (page 10)

8–10 oz. white ready-to-roll fondant icing

yellow food coloring paste

½ quantity Royal Icing (page 13)

black food coloring paste

confectioners' sugar, for dusting

1 tablespoon sieved apricot jam, warmed

4–5-inch sunflower-shaped cookie cutter

2 baking sheets, lined with baking parchment

small piping bag with a small star-shaped tip

makes about 12 depending on size

You should have rolled out the Basic Vanilla Cookie dough to a thickness of ⅛ inch on a lightly floured work surface. Using the sunflower cookie cutter, carefully stamp out shapes. Arrange them on the prepared baking sheets. Gather together the scraps of the dough and re-roll to make more shapes. Refrigerate for 15 minutes.

Preheat the oven to 350°F.

Bake the cookies on the middle shelf of the preheated oven for about 12 minutes, or until golden, swapping the sheets around if needed. Let cool on the trays for 5 minutes before transferring to a wire rack to cool completely.

Tint the fondant icing yellow (see page 16 for help on tinting) using the yellow food coloring paste and the Royal Icing black using the black food coloring paste.

Now see opposite for instructions on how to decorate the cookies.

1

2

how to decorate
sunflowers

✳ Lightly dust a work surface with confectioners' sugar. Roll out the yellow fondant icing to a thickness of 1⁄16 inch.

✳ Using the sunflower cookie cutter again, stamp out flowers to match each of your cookies. Lightly brush the top of each cold cookie with the warmed apricot jam. Carefully position one fondant flower on top of each cookie, gently smoothing into place with your hands. You might find it easier to transfer the fondant flower while it's still in the cutter. **(1)**

✳ Fill the piping bag with the black royal icing and pipe rosettes into the middle of each sunflower. **(2)**

✳ Allow to set before serving.

Watch out! Here's an invasion of edible bugs and critters that kids will love to help decorate. Let them loose with the piping bag and food coloring (within reason!), and let them design their own critters.

garden critters

1 quantity Basic Vanilla Cookies (page 10)

1 quantity Royal Icing (page 13)

food coloring pastes in assorted colors

critter-shaped cookie cutters (e.g. snail, ladybug, butterfly, caterpillar)

2 baking sheets, lined with baking parchment

small piping bag with a fine writing tip, or make your own (see page 15)

mini palette knife or small knife

makes about 12—18 depending on size

You should have rolled out the Basic Vanilla Cookie dough to a thickness of ⅛ inch on a lightly floured work surface. Using the critter cookie cutters, carefully stamp out shapes. Arrange them on the prepared baking sheets. Gather together the scraps of the dough and re-roll to make more shapes. Refrigerate for 15 minutes.

Preheat the oven to 350°F.

Bake the cookies on the middle shelf of the preheated oven for about 12 minutes, or until golden, swapping the sheets around if needed. Let cool on the sheets for about 5 minutes before transferring to a wire rack to cool completely.

Divide the Royal Icing between the number of bowls you need for your colors of icing. Tint each one a different color (see page 16 for help on tinting) using the food coloring pastes.

Fill the piping bag with whichever color you want to start with. Pipe borders around the cold cookies. "Flood" the area inside the borders with icing (see page 44 for step pictures of "flooding"): once you have made a neat border, you can spoon icing within the borders and spread it carefully up to the edges with a mini palette knife or small knife.

Let it dry and harden slightly before you pipe any lines or other features on top of the flooded icing. Allow to set before serving.

This simple shortbread can be adapted into a variety of flavors and colors. Match the color of the sugar to the flavor of the cookies: yellow for lemon, green for pistachio, and purple for lavender. Decide on one flavor and corresponding color scheme before you start.

15 tablespoons unsalted butter, softened

⅔ cup sugar

1 egg, beaten

1 teaspoon pure vanilla extract

2⅓ cups all-purpose flour, plus extra for dusting

a pinch of salt

¼ cup granulated sugar

yellow, red, green, and/or purple food coloring pastes to match your color scheme

1 tablespoon milk

**one flavoring of
your choice**

2 tablespoons finely chopped mixed peel or 4 oz. chopped glacé cherries or 4 oz. chopped pistachios or 2 tablespoons dried lavender flowers, to match your color scheme

*2 baking sheets, lined with
baking parchment*

makes about 20

sugared refrigerator cookies

Cream together the butter and sugar until light and creamy in the bowl of a freestanding mixer (or use an electric whisk and mixing bowl). Add the egg and vanilla and mix well. Sift the flour and salt into the mixture, along with the flavoring you have chosen, and mix again until smooth and the flour is incorporated.

Tip the dough onto a very lightly floured work surface and divide into 2. Roll each piece of dough into a sausage shape roughly 2 inches in diameter, wrap tightly in waxed paper, and refrigerate until solid—at least 2 hours.

Preheat the oven to 300°F.

Tip the granulated sugar into a plastic food bag. Using the tip of a wooden skewer, gradually add the color of food coloring paste you have chosen to match the flavor of the cookie, mixing well until the desired shade is reached. Tip the colored sugar onto a baking sheet. Remove the cookie dough logs from the refrigerator and brush them with the milk. Roll in the colored sugar to coat evenly.

Using a sharp knife, cut the logs into ⅜-inch slices and arrange on the prepared baking sheets. Bake on the middle shelf of the preheated oven for about 15 minutes, or until pale golden. Let cool on the sheets for 5 minutes before transferring to a wire rack to cool completely.

1 2 3

These cookies make beautiful wedding favors. They are best made from simple shapes: squares, rounds, or hearts all work well. Frost the cookies in colors to match the wedding color scheme and design. Why not personalize them for each guest and use as place settings?

monogrammed wedding cookies

1 quantity Basic Vanilla Cookies (page 10)

1 quantity Royal Icing (page 13)

blue food coloring paste (or whichever color you need for your color scheme)

square, round, and/or heart-shaped cookie cutters

2 baking sheets, lined with baking parchment

small piping bag with a fine writing tip, or make your own (see page 15)

mini palette knife or small knife

makes about 12—18 depending on size

You should have rolled out the Basic Vanilla Cookie dough to a thickness of ⅛ inch on a lightly floured work surface. Using the cookie cutters, carefully stamp out shapes. Arrange them on the prepared baking sheets. Gather together the scraps of the dough and re-roll to make more shapes. Refrigerate for 15 minutes.

Preheat the oven to 350°F.

Bake the cookies on the middle shelf of the preheated oven for about 12 minutes, or until golden, swapping the sheets around if needed. Let cool on the sheets for about 5 minutes before transferring to a wire rack to cool completely.

Divide the Royal Icing between 2 bowls. Tint one blue (see page 16 for help on tinting) using the food coloring paste. Leave the second bowl of icing white.

Fill the piping bag with whichever color you want to start with. Pipe borders around the cold cookies. **(1)** Once you have made a neat border, you can spoon icing within the borders and spread it carefully up to the edges with a mini palette knife or small knife. This is called "flooding." **(2)** Let it dry and harden slightly.

Now fill your clean piping bag with the other color of icing. Pipe lines, dots, or other simple decorations on the cookies, then your chosen monogram in the center. **(3)** Allow to set before serving.

These elegant cookies are a breeze to make and wouldn't look out of place at the smartest tea table. The dough can be prepared in advance and the cookies baked off the day before you plan to decorate them. The feathering technique is useful to know because it can be used for royal icing as well as this chocolate glaze. Feel free to be as expressive as you like with the flourishes. I have made these cookies in different-sized rounds, but they could easily be stamped into hearts or squares.

black and white cookies

1⅓ cups all-purpose flour, plus extra for dusting

⅓ cup unsweetened cocoa powder

½ teaspoon baking powder

½ teaspoon baking soda

a pinch of salt

1 stick unsalted butter, softened

1 cup plus 2 tablespoons sugar

1 egg, beaten

1 teaspoon pure vanilla extract

to decorate

3½ oz. white chocolate, chopped

1 quantity Chocolate Glaze (page 12)

2-inch and 3-inch round cookie cutters

2 baking sheets, lined with baking parchment

small piping bag with a fine writing tip, or make your own (see page 15)

mini palette knife or small knife

makes about 16

Sift together the flour, cocoa powder, baking powder, baking soda, and salt into a mixing bowl.

Cream together the butter and sugar until light and creamy in the bowl of a freestanding mixer (or use an electric whisk and mixing bowl). Add the beaten egg and vanilla and mix well. Add the sifted dry ingredients and mix again until smooth. Bring together into a dough and knead very lightly and briefly. Flatten into a disk, wrap in plastic wrap, and refrigerate for a couple of hours until very firm.

When you are ready to start baking, preheat the oven to 350°F.

Dust the work surface with flour and roll out the chilled cookie dough to a thickness of about ⅛ inch. Using the cookie cutters, carefully stamp out rounds. Arrange them on the prepared baking sheets. Gather together the scraps of the dough and re-roll to make more rounds.

Bake on the middle shelf of the preheated oven for 12–15 minutes, or until crisp. Let cool on the sheets for a couple of minutes before transferring to a wire rack to cool completely.

To decorate the cookies, put the white chocolate in a heatproof bowl set over a pan of barely simmering water. Stir until smooth and thoroughly melted. Put the cookies back on some baking parchment to catch any drips while you are decorating them.

Fill your piping bag with the molten white chocolate and get a wooden skewer or toothpick ready for the feathering.

Now see overleaf for instructions on how to decorate the cookies.

1

2

how to decorate
black and white cookies

❋ Pour some of the Chocolate Glaze over each cookie with a spoon **(1)**.

❋ Spread the glaze neatly over the cookie, just to the edge, with the back of the spoon or with a mini palette knife. Repeat with the remaining cookies **(2)**.

❋ Working quickly, pipe dots of white chocolate over the dark chocolate glaze on just a few of the cookies **(3)**.

❋ Using the point of a wooden skewer or toothpick, drag the white chocolate into the chocolate glaze to create a feathered effect. Repeat with the remaining cookies and let set before serving **(4)**.

3

These elegant and sophisticated cookies look like they belong in a chic Parisian pâtisserie, but are actually incredibly easy to make. They can be tinted almost any color imaginable and filled with jam, cream, buttercream, or ganache.

macaroons

1 cup confectioners' sugar

½ cup ground almonds

3 egg whites

a pinch of salt

a pinch of cream of tartar

¼ cup sugar

pink food coloring paste

green food coloring paste

yellow food coloring paste

1 tablespoon unsweetened cocoa powder

1 quantity Vanilla Buttercream (page 12—vanilla or flavored with lemon, pistachio, etc. to suit your color scheme), Chocolate Ganache (page 12), whipped heavy cream, or jam

4 small piping bags with ⅜-inch plain tips

2 baking sheets, lined with baking parchment

makes about 20

Preheat the oven to 325°F.

Sift the confectioners' sugar and ground almonds together into a bowl.

Put the egg whites in the bowl of a freestanding electric mixer fitted with the whisk attachment (or use an electric whisk and mixing bowl). Add the salt and cream of tartar and whisk until the egg whites form soft peaks. Add the sugar a teaspoon at a time, whisking well between each addition. Continue whisking until the mixture is stiff and glossy.

Fold the confectioners' sugar and ground almonds into the mixture using a large metal spoon. Divide the mixture between 4 bowls and tint 3 of them a different color using the food coloring pastes and a wooden skewer or toothpick. Fold in gently until evenly dyed. Stir the cocoa powder into the fourth bowl.

Fill each piping bag with a different color of macaroon mixture. Pipe 2-inch disks onto the prepared baking sheets. Sharply tap the sheet on the work surface—this will knock any extra air bubbles out of the macaroons. Set aside for 10 minutes to allow the mixture to settle before baking.

Bake on the middle shelf of the preheated oven for 8–9 minutes. Let cool on the sheets for 5 minutes before transferring to a wire rack to cool completely.

Sandwich the macaroons together with your choice of buttercream, Chocolate Ganache, whipped cream, or jam and serve immediately.

This is the kind of treat to put a smile on your face—it has something to do with the nostalgic combination of chocolate, peppermint, and jimmies. You could also try dipping just the top cookie in chocolate glaze and coating in sprinkles too.

mint chocolate kisses

6 oz. bittersweet chocolate, chopped

12 tablespoons unsalted butter

2 medium eggs

1 cup plus 2 tablespoons packed light muscovado sugar

2 cups self-rising flour

¾ teaspoon baking powder

a pinch of salt

minty buttercream

5 tablespoons unsalted butter, softened

1 cup confectioners' sugar, sifted

½–1 teaspoon peppermint extract

to decorate

6½ oz. bittersweet chocolate, chopped

jimmies

2 baking sheets, lined with baking parchment

makes about 18

Put the chocolate and butter in a heatproof bowl set over a pan of barely simmering water. Stir until smooth and thoroughly combined.

Put the eggs and sugar in the bowl of a freestanding electric mixer fitted with the whisk attachment (or use an electric whisk and mixing bowl) and beat until pale and light. Add the chocolate mixture and mix until smooth.

Sift together the flour, baking powder, and salt. Add to the mixing bowl and stir until smooth. Bring together into a dough, cover, and refrigerate for a couple of hours.

When you are ready to start baking, preheat the oven to 350°F.

Remove the cookie dough from the refrigerator and pull off walnut-sized pieces. Roll into balls and arrange on the prepared baking sheets. Bake in batches on the middle shelf of the preheated oven for about 12 minutes, or until the cookies are crisp on the edges but slightly soft in the middle. Let cool on the sheets for a few minutes before transferring to a wire rack to cool completely.

To make the minty buttercream, put the butter in a large bowl and, using a freestanding mixer or electric whisk, cream until really soft. Gradually add the sifted confectioners' sugar and beat until pale and smooth. Add peppermint to taste.

Sandwich the cold cookies together with the minty buttercream.

To decorate, put the chocolate in a heatproof bowl set over a pan of barely simmering water. Stir until smooth and melted. Let cool slightly. Half-dip the cookies in the melted chocolate, sprinkle with jimmies, and allow to set on baking parchment before serving.

small cakes

I would love someone forever if they were to make a tray of these for me! Paper cupcake cases come in hundreds of colors and designs, and the choice available for Valentine's cupcakes is vast—look out for polka dots, love hearts, and foil cases in shiny red and pink. Red velvet cake is not just for Valentine's, but made in miniature and topped with sparkly red marzipan hearts, it's a marriage made in cupcake heaven.

red velvet valentine's cupcakes

1¾ cups all-purpose flour

1 teaspoon baking soda

2 heaping tablespoons unsweetened cocoa powder

a pinch of salt

15 tablespoons unsalted butter, softened

1 cup sugar

2 eggs, beaten

1 teaspoon pure vanilla extract

1 cup buttermilk, at room temperature

1 teaspoon red food coloring paste (ruby or Christmas red is best)

1 quantity Marshmallow Frosting (page 11)

marzipan hearts

6½ oz. natural marzipan

red food coloring paste (ruby or Christmas red is best)

edible red glitter

1–2 muffin pans, lined with paper cupcake cases

makes 18

Preheat the oven to 350°F.

Sift together the flour, baking soda, cocoa powder, and salt in a mixing bowl.

Cream together the butter and sugar until light and creamy in the bowl of a freestanding mixer (or use an electric whisk and mixing bowl). Gradually add the beaten eggs, mixing well between each addition and scraping down the side of the mixing bowl from time to time. Add the vanilla.

With the mixer on low speed, add the sifted dry ingredients to the mixture, alternating with the buttermilk. Mix until smooth, then add the red food coloring paste—you will need to add enough to make the mixture deep red and the quantity needed may vary depending on the brand and color used. Stir until evenly mixed.

Divide the mixture between the paper cupcake cases, filling them two-thirds full, and bake on the middle shelf of the preheated oven for 20 minutes, or until well risen and a skewer inserted into the middle of the cupcakes comes out clean. Let cool in the pans for 5 minutes before transferring to a wire rack to cool completely.

Spoon the Marshmallow Frosting on top of the cold cupcakes, swirling and shaping it with the back of a spoon to get a lovely peaked effect.

Now see overleaf for instructions on how to make the marzipan hearts.

1

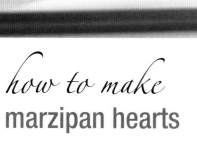

2

how to make
marzipan hearts

✳ Tint the marzipan red (see page 16 for help on tinting) using the food coloring paste.

✳ Make one heart at a time. Break off a small piece of marzipan and roll into a cylinder in the palm of your hand. **(1)**

✳ Gently squeeze the ends toward each other to make the top of the heart. **(2)**

✳ Using your fingers, squeeze the other end into a point to make the bottom of the heart. **(3)**

✳ Put on baking parchment and repeat to make more hearts in assorted sizes. Dust with edible red glitter. **(4)**

✳ Sit the hearts on top of the frosted cupcakes just before serving.

3

These delicately spiced little cakes are topped with maple syrup-flavored cream cheese frosting and then adorned with a wafer-thin slice of candied pear and a cluster of caramelized nuts. The candied pears can be made in advance and stored on baking parchment in a cool, dry place until ready to serve.

fall spiced honey cakes

12 tablespoons unsalted butter, softened

½ cup packed light muscovado sugar

⅓ cup honey

3 eggs, beaten

1⅓ cups all-purpose flour

3 teaspoons baking powder

2 teaspoons ground ginger

1 teaspoon ground cinnamon

a pinch of ground allspice

a pinch of salt

finely grated zest of ½ orange

finely grated zest of ½ unwaxed lemon

2 tablespoons freshly squeezed orange juice

Cream Cheese Frosting (page 13 and made with maple syrup instead of honey)

candied nuts

¾ cup sugar

3½ oz. mixed shelled nuts, lightly toasted

pear wafers

¼ cup sugar

freshly squeezed juice of ½ lemon

3 firm pears, e.g. Bartlett

1–2 muffin pans, lined with paper cupcake cases

1 baking sheet, oiled

1–2 baking sheets, lined with baking parchment

makes 12

Preheat the oven to 350°F.

Cream together the butter, sugar, and honey until light and creamy in the bowl of a freestanding mixer (or use an electric whisk and mixing bowl). Gradually add the beaten eggs, mixing well between each addition and scraping down the side of the mixing bowl from time to time.

Sift together the flour, baking powder, spices, and salt. Add to the cake mixture and mix until thoroughly combined. Add the grated orange and lemon zest and orange juice and mix again.

Divide the mixture between the paper cupcake cases, filling them two-thirds full, and bake on the middle shelf of the preheated oven for 20–25 minutes, or until well risen and a skewer inserted into the middle of the cupcakes comes out clean. Let cool in the pans for 5 minutes before transferring to a wire rack to cool completely.

To make the candied nuts, put the sugar and 3 tablespoons water in a saucepan over low/medium heat. Leave until the sugar has completely dissolved, then raise the heat and bring the syrup to a steady boil. Continue to cook without stirring until the syrup turns a deep amber color. Working quickly, tip the toasted nuts into the syrup and stir to coat. Using 2 spoons, divide the candied nuts into 12 piles (one for each cupcake) on the oiled baking sheet. Allow to cool and harden.

To make the pear wafers, preheat the oven to 225°F.

Put the sugar, 6 tablespoons water, and lemon juice in a small saucepan and bring to a boil. Simmer for 2 minutes, then remove from the heat and let cool. Slice the pears no thicker than ⅛ inch—this is easiest using a mandoline slicer. Dip each slice into the syrup and shake off any excess. Lay the pears in a single layer on the lined baking sheets and bake on the middle and lower shelves of the oven for about 2 hours, or until beginning to crisp up and turn golden. Turn the slices over on the parchment and, if using 2, swap the sheets around halfway through cooking. Allow to cool—they will crisp up further as they cool.

When the cupcakes, candied nuts, and pear wafers are all cold, spread the Cream Cheese Frosting over the cupcakes and decorate with a pile of candied nuts and a single pear wafer.

Here's an idea for the child in all of us! You can really go to town with the decorating and pick any animal that has distinctive enough features to represent in sprinkles, candies, and colored frosting. I've made a rabbit, monkey, teddy bear, and pig, but the choice is yours.

animal-face cupcakes

1 quantity Buttermilk Cake (page 9)

1 quantity Meringue Buttercream (page 11)

to decorate

food coloring pastes in assorted colors

2½ oz. bittersweet chocolate, chopped

marshmallows in assorted sizes and colors

jelly beans in assorted colors

licorice strips

white, milk, and bittersweet chocolate buttons in assorted sizes

chocolate jimmies and other sprinkles

white sugar strands or nonpareils

a little Royal Icing (page 13)

1–2 muffin pans, lined with paper cupcake cases

small piping bag with a fine writing tip, or make your own (see page 15)

makes 12—16

Preheat the oven to 350°F.

Divide the Buttermilk Cake mixture between the paper cupcake cases, filling them two-thirds full, and bake on the middle shelf of the preheated oven for 20 minutes, or until well risen and a skewer inserted into the middle of the cupcakes comes out clean. Let cool in the pans for 5 minutes before transferring to a wire rack to cool completely.

How you decorate these cupakes depends on the animals you have chosen. These are just tips for making facial features.

Tint the Meringue Buttercream into as many different colors as you need by dividing it between separate bowls and tinting each one using food coloring pastes (see page 16 for help on tinting).

To make a teddy bear, monkey, or any other brown animal face, put the chocolate in a heatproof bowl set over a pan of barely simmering water. Stir until smooth and melted. Add to one bowl of meringue buttercream and stir until well mixed.

Cover the tops of the cold cupcakes in your tinted buttercream, spreading smoothly with a palette knife.

Use marshmallows in assorted sizes to make noses and snouts. Cover with tinted buttercream to match the rest of the face and push into the face to attach. You can also cut a large marshmallow in half and pinch or squash with your fingers to shape into ears. Stick at the top of the cupcake.

Use halved jelly beans for nostrils or large eyes. Strips of licorice positioned under the nose make good mouths or whiskers.

Use white, milk, and bittersweet chocolate buttons, individually or stacked, for ears. Stick in place with a dab of buttercream.

Chocolate jimmies and other sprinkles and nonpareils make ideal fur, while sugar strands can be used for buck teeth.

Complete the features with thinly piped black Royal Icing to make little eyes and dainty smiles or just to glue features in place.

The crystallized flowers on these delicate cupcakes are truly stunning and very easy to make. They do need at least 12 hours to dry properly, but once you've made them they will keep for up to 4 days in a cool, dry place. I have used 4–5 spring flowers per cake, but you could use fewer (and of different varieties) if you prefer.

spring flower cupcakes

1 quantity Buttermilk Cake (page 9)
1 quantity Meringue Buttercream (page 11)
pink food coloring paste
yellow food coloring paste
lilac food coloring paste

crystallized flowers
fresh primroses
fresh violets and violas
1 egg white
⅔ cup superfine sugar

1–2 muffin pans, lined with paper cupcake cases

makes 12–16

Make the crystallized flowers the day before you plan to serve these cupcakes. See overleaf for instructions on how to make the crystallized flowers.

Preheat the oven to 350°F.

Divide the Buttermilk Cake mixture between the paper cupcake cases, filling them two-thirds full, and bake on the middle shelf of the preheated oven for 20 minutes, or until well risen and a skewer inserted into the middle of the cupcakes comes out clean. Let cool in the pans for 5 minutes before transferring to a wire rack to cool completely.

Divide the Meringue Buttercream between 3 bowls and tint each one a different color (see page 16 for help on tinting) using the food coloring pastes. Tint them the shade you like by very gradually adding more coloring.

Spread the buttercream over the cold cupcakes and arrange the crystallized flowers on top.

how to crystallize
flowers and petals

❋ This is a very simple and beautiful way to decorate cakes. Make sure that the flowers you choose are not poisonous, are unsprayed, and are clean and dry.

❋ If you are using whole flowers like primroses, violets, and violas, snip the flowers off the stems, leaving just a small bit of the stem.

❋ If you are using rose petals, carefully pull the petals off the flower heads.

❋ Very lightly beat 1 egg white with a fork until it is only just foamy (this will only take about 5 seconds). Put a few tablespoons of superfine sugar in a bowl.

❋ Crystallize one petal (or flower) at a time. Use a pastry brush to lightly coat both sides of the petal with the egg white. **(1)**

❋ Sprinkle the wet petal with superfine sugar all over (both sides) until evenly coated in sugar. **(2)**

❋ Arrange the petals in a single layer on a wire rack lined with baking parchment and let dry for at least 1 hour, but preferably up to 12 hours. The petals shouldn't touch while they are drying. **(3)**

❋ Flowers and petals will keep for up to 4 days, but are best used on the day they are ready as the natural color will fade over time.

❋ As well as flowers and petals, you can also crystallize strands of red, white, and black currants. Follow the same method as for the flowers above.

3½ oz. chocolate, chopped

1⅔ cups all-purpose flour

⅓ cup unsweetened cocoa powder

1 tablespoon baking powder

a pinch of salt

13 tablespoons unsalted butter, softened

1 cup light muscovado sugar

4 eggs, beaten

1 teaspoon pure vanilla extract

¼ cup sour cream, at room temperature

to decorate

¼ cup sieved apricot jam, warmed

chocolate truffles

1 quantity Chocolate Ganache (page 12)

storebought crystallized violets and roses, edible gold and silver leaf, chocolate-coated coffee beans, chopped pistachio nuts, and/or melted white chocolate

8 x 12-inch baking pan, greased and lined with baking parchment

small square, round, and triangular cookie cutters

makes 16–20

This neat idea looks tricky, but in reality it's easy as can be. Why not serve this box of chocolates after a smart dinner—it's dessert and petits fours all rolled into one.

box of chocolates

Preheat the oven to 350°F.

Put the chocolate in a heatproof bowl set over a pan of barely simmering water. Stir until smooth and thoroughly melted.

Sift together the flour, cocoa powder, baking powder, and salt.

Cream together the butter and sugar until light and creamy in the bowl of a freestanding mixer (or use an electric whisk and mixing bowl). Gradually add the beaten eggs, mixing well between each addition and scraping down the side of the mixing bowl from time to time. Add the vanilla and melted chocolate.

With the mixer on low speed, add the sifted dry ingredients to the mixture, alternating with the sour cream.

Pour the mixture into the prepared baking pan, spread level, and bake on the middle shelf of the preheated oven for 20–25 minutes, or until a skewer inserted into the middle of the cake comes out clean. Let cool in the pan for 10 minutes before transferring to a wire rack to cool completely.

Refer to the step instructions on the page opposite for decorating the chocolates.

how to decorate
the chocolates

✳ Stamp out shapes from the cold cake using the shaped cookie cutters. **(1)**

✳ Brush the tops and sides with the warmed apricot jam and set the little cakes on a wire rack.

✳ You can pop a chocolate truffle on top of some of the little cakes to make a bump.

✳ Spoon the Chocolate Ganache over the cakes, spreading it evenly with a palette knife and letting it drip down. **(2)**

✳ Allow to set for 20 minutes, then decorate with the toppings, such as crystallized violets and roses, edible gold or silver leaf, chocolate-coated coffee beans, chopped pistachio nuts, and melted white chocolate drizzled over with a piping bag. **(3)**

These cupcakes have hidden jewels in the mixture—nuggets of almonds, dried cranberries, and white chocolate chips—and they are topped with a snowdrift of meringue frosting. Make the sugar-paste snowflakes a couple of days before serving and set aside to dry before decorating with royal icing and assorted sprinkles and glitter.

snowflake cupcakes

⅓ cup blanched almonds, chopped

1⅓ cups all-purpose flour

1 tablespoon baking powder

a pinch of salt

12 tablespoons unsalted butter, softened

¾ cup plus 2 tablespoons sugar

3 eggs, beaten

2 teaspoons pure vanilla extract

3 tablespoons sour cream or milk, at room temperature

⅔ cup white chocolate chips

½ cup dried cranberries

white nonpareils

1 quantity Marshmallow Frosting (page 11)

edible glitter and luster dust in silver and white

snowflakes

confectioners' sugar, for dusting

8 oz. white sugar paste

½ quantity Royal Icing (page 13)

small snowflake-shaped cutter

1–2 muffin pans, lined with paper cupcake cases

small piping bag with a fine writing tip, or make your own (see page 15)

makes 12–16

Make the snowflakes the day before you make the cupcakes. Lightly dust a clean, dry work surface with confectioners' sugar. Roll the sugar paste out to a thickness of no more than ⅛ inch. Using the snowflake cutter, stamp out the desired number of shapes. Set aside on baking parchment to dry out overnight.

The next day, fill the piping bag with the Royal Icing and pipe little dots onto the sugar-paste snowflakes. Sprinkle with edible glitter and/or luster dust and let set.

When you are ready to bake the cupcakes, preheat the oven to 350°F.

Put the almonds on a baking sheet and toast in the preheated oven for 5–7 minutes, or until just turning golden. Remove from the oven and let cool.

Sift together the flour, baking powder, and salt.

Cream together the butter and sugar until light and creamy in the bowl of a freestanding mixer (or use an electric whisk and mixing bowl). Gradually add the beaten eggs, mixing well between each addition and scraping down the side of the mixing bowl from time to time. Add the vanilla.

Add the sifted dry ingredients to the mixture and mix until just incorporated. Stir in the sour cream. Fold in the almonds, chocolate chips, and cranberries.

Divide the mixture between the paper cupcake cases, filling them two-thirds full, and bake on the middle shelf of the preheated oven for 20–25 minutes, or until well risen and a skewer inserted into the middle of the cupcakes comes out clean. Let cool in the pans for 5 minutes before transferring to a wire rack to cool completely.

Tip the white nonpareils into a bowl or saucer. Frost the cupcakes with the Marshmallow Frosting and decorate the edges with the nonpareils, using the instructions on page 18. Scatter some edible glitter and/or luster dust over the top and finish off each cupcake with a sugar-paste snowflake.

Who doesn't love carrot cake? This light, moist recipe is made more delicious with the addition of coconut and marmalade. The marzipan carrots and rabbits can be made days in advance and will keep well in an airtight box. However, be sure to place them on top of the cakes just before serving, otherwise the food coloring will bleed into the frosting.

carrot cake cupcakes

1¾ cups all-purpose flour

1 teaspoon baking powder

½ teaspoon baking soda

½ teaspoon ground cinnamon, plus extra for dusting

2 eggs

1 cup packed light brown sugar

⅔ cup peanut oil

1 teaspooon pure vanilla extract

2 tablespoons fine-cut orange marmalade

⅓ cup shelled walnuts or pecans, toasted

1 cup grated carrots

⅓ cup desiccated coconut

1 egg white

1 quantity Cream Cheese Frosting (page 13)

carrots and rabbits

10 oz. natural marzipan

orange food coloring paste

brown food coloring paste

white mini-marshmallows

white sugar strands

angelica

1–2 muffin pans, lined with paper cupcake cases

makes 16—18

Start making the marzipan carrots the day before you make the cupcakes. Tint two-thirds of the marzipan orange using the orange food coloring paste (see page 16 for help on tinting). Tint it the shade of orange you like by very gradually adding more coloring. Break off small nuggets of the marzipan and roll between your hands to make carrot shapes. Using the blunt end of a wooden skewer, push a small hole into the top of each carrot.

Use the remaining marzipan to make the rabbits. Tint it brown using the brown food coloring paste. Break off small nuggets of marzipan and roll between your hands for the rabbits' bodies, and do the same with smaller pieces for the heads. Carefully press a head onto a body. Make tiny ears from the marzipan and carefully attach to the top of each rabbit head. Dip the tip of a wooden skewer into the brown food coloring paste and paint eyes, a nose, and a mouth onto each rabbit. Attach a mini-marshmallow for a fluffy tail and use the white sugar strands to make the rabbits' teeth. Now let the rabbits and carrots dry out overnight on a sheet of baking parchment in an airtight box.

The next day, cut the angelica into very fine matchsticks about ½ inch long and push into the small hole in the top of each carrot. When you are ready to make the cupcakes, preheat the oven to 350°F.

Sift together the flour, baking powder, baking soda, and cinnamon. In another bowl, whisk together the whole eggs, sugar, oil, vanilla, and marmalade. Add the nuts, grated carrots, and coconut and mix again.

Add the sifted dry ingredients and mix lightly. Put the egg white in a grease-free bowl and whisk until it forms stiff peaks, then gently fold into the mixture.

Divide the mixture between the paper cupcake cases, filling them three-quarters full, and bake in the preheated oven for 25 minutes, or until well risen and a skewer inserted into the middle of the cupcakes comes out clean. Let cool in the pans for 5 minutes before transferring to a wire rack to cool completely.

Spread the Cream Cheese Frosting over the cold cupcakes, dust with cinnamon, and arrange the marzipan carrots and rabbits on top.

This is an edible festive wreath to take center stage for a Christmas afternoon tea. Make the cupcakes in silver and gold cases in an assortment of sizes. The white and bittersweet chocolate leaves can be made in advance and kept in a cool, dry place until required.

christmas wreath

1 quantity Buttermilk Cake (page 9)

1 quantity Meringue Buttercream (page 11)

red sugar-coated candies

edible gold and silver glitter

chocolate leaves

6½ oz. white chocolate, chopped

6½ oz. bittersweet chocolate, chopped

fresh bay leaves

muffin pan, lined with 8–10 silver or gold paper cupcake cases

mini muffin pan, lined with 8–10 silver or gold paper cases in the coordinating size

makes 1 large wreath

Preheat the oven to 350°F.

Divide the Buttermilk Cake mixture between the paper cases, filling them two-thirds full, and bake on the middle shelf of the preheated oven for 12–25 minutes. The time will vary according to the size of the cakes—keep an eye on them and take them out when they are well risen and a skewer inserted into the middle of the cakes comes out clean. Let cool in the pans for 5 minutes before transferring to a wire rack to cool completely.

While the cakes are cooling, make the chocolate leaves. You will need about 40 leaves, so these can be done in batches. Refer to the step instructions overleaf for making the chocolate leaves.

Spread the Meringue Buttercream over the cold cakes and arrange the cakes in a circle on a large serving platter. Decorate each cake with the white and bittersweet chocolate leaves. Scatter over the red candies to look like berries and dust with edible gold and silver glitter.

melting chocolate

Weigh out the required amount of chocolate and chop into small pieces. Put it in a clean, dry heatproof bowl and sit over a pan of barely simmering water. Do not allow the bottom of the bowl to touch the water. Once the chocolate is half melted, you can remove the pan from the heat and allow the chocolate to melt slowly. Stir until smooth before using.

how to make
chocolate leaves

✳ Wash and thoroughly dry the bay leaves.

✳ Melt the white and bittersweet chocolate separately as described on the opposite page.

✳ Using a clean, dry pastry brush, spread a thin, even layer of melted chocolate over one side of the bay leaves. Allow to set. **(1)**

✳ Repeat with a second layer of chocolate.

✳ Once all the chocolate has set, very carefully peel off the leaves. **(2)** Repeat as necessary to make enough leaves.

✳ You can make chocolate leaves from other fresh, firm leaves, but make sure they are not poisonous.

✳ You can also make simple shapes such as stars using melted chocolate. Melt the chocolate as described on the page opposite, fill a small piping bag with it and pipe star shapes onto baking parchment. Allow to set until firm, then carefully peel off and use to decorate cupcakes.

✳ See also page 121 for instructions on making chocolate sheets to cut into panels and other shapes.

Each of these little cakes is topped with meringue buttercream and a selection of candies and sprinkles in all the colors of the rainbow. If you had a very large serving dish you could arrange the cupcakes in a rainbow shape. They're perfect for a children's party—you could even get the kids to decorate their own at the party.

a rainbow of cupcakes

1 quantity Buttermilk Cake (page 9)

1 quantity Meringue Buttercream (page 11)

food coloring pastes in all colors, e.g. red, orange, yellow, green, blue, indigo, and violet

little candies in colors to match your food coloring pastes

1–2 muffin pans, lined with paper cupcake cases

makes 12—16

Preheat the oven to 350°F.

Divide the Buttermilk Cake mixture between the paper cupcake cases, filling them two-thirds full, and bake on the middle shelf of the preheated oven for 20 minutes, or until well risen and a skewer inserted into the middle of the cupcakes comes out clean. Let cool in the pans for 5 minutes before transferring to a wire rack to cool completely.

Divide the Meringue Buttercream between 7 bowls (or however many you need for the colors you're using) and tint each one a different color (see page 16 for help on tinting) using the food coloring pastes. Tint them the shade you like by very gradually adding more coloring.

Spread the buttercream over the cold cupcakes and arrange the coordinating candies on top.

A step up from the more traditional butterfly fairy cakes you might have made with your mom when you were little, these have painted sugar-paste wings to make them look ready for flight! Once you have mastered the technique for making and painting the wings, you can let your imagination run wild with colors and patterns.

butterfly cupcakes

1 quantity Buttermilk Cake (page 9)

1 quantity Meringue Buttercream (page 11)

jimmies

butterflies

confectioners' sugar, for dusting

9 oz. white sugar paste

1 quantity Royal Icing (page 13)

pink food coloring paste

yellow food coloring paste

brown food coloring paste

1–2 muffin pans, lined with paper cupcake cases

butterfly shaped cutter

small piping bag with a fine writing tip, or make your own (see page 15)

mini palette knife or small knife

makes 12—16

Preheat the oven to 350°F.

Divide the Buttermilk Cake mixture between the paper cupcake cases, filling them two-thirds full, and bake on the middle shelf of the preheated oven for 20 minutes, or until well risen and a skewer inserted into the middle of the cupcakes comes out clean. Let cool in the pans for 5 minutes before transferring to a wire rack to cool completely.

Spread the Meringue Buttercream over the cold cupcakes and scatter the jimmies over them.

Get your butterfly cutter, piping bag, and a wooden skewer or toothpick ready.

Refer to the step instructions overleaf for making the sugar-paste butterflies.

When the butterflies are completely dry, place matching pairs of wings on the cupcakes, pushing them at an angle into the topping.

how to make
sugar-paste butterflies

※ Lightly dust a clean, dry work surface with confectioners' sugar. Roll the sugar paste out to a thickness of no more than ⅛ inch.

※ Using the butterfly-shaped cutter, stamp out the desired number of shapes. **(1)**

※ Cut each butterfly in half through the body to create 2 wings and set aside on baking parchment to dry out overnight. **(2)**

※ Divide the Royal Icing between 3 bowls. Tint one pink and one yellow (see page 16 for help on tinting) using the food coloring pastes. Tint them the shade of pink or yellow you like by very gradually adding more coloring. Leave the third bowl of icing white.

※ Pour 2–3 tablespoons of the white icing into your piping bag.

※ Working on one wing at a time, pipe a border around the wing. "Flood" the inner half of the wing, nearest the butterfly's body, with white icing (see page 44 for step pictures of "flooding") by spreading it to the inner edge with the mini palette knife or small knife.

※ Fill the other half of the wing with either pink or yellow icing, spreading to the outer edge and inward to meet the white icing. **(3)**

※ Using the tip of the skewer, drag the colored icing into the white to create a feathered effect. **(4)** Leave to dry. Repeat with the remaining wings.

※ Tint a small amount of the white icing brown and use to pipe a small line down the middle of each wing to create the body. **(5)**

※ Allow the wings to dry completely.

1

Topped with a cascade of summer berries and a swirl of strawberry-scented, delicate pink buttercream, these cupcakes are the height of summer sophistication. You could also top the cakes with just one type of fruit if you prefer. Check out the suppliers on page 126 for the prettiest paper cases to complete the picture.

summer berry cupcakes

1 quantity Buttermilk Cake (page 9)

1 quantity Meringue Buttercream (page 11)

3–4 tablespoons sieved strawberry jam

assorted summer berries, e.g. strawberries, raspberries, blueberries, and red currants

confectioners' sugar, for dusting

1–2 muffin pans, lined with paper cupcake cases

makes 12—16

Preheat the oven to 350°F.

Divide the Buttermilk Cake mixture between the paper cupcake cases, filling them two-thirds full, and bake on the middle shelf of the preheated oven for 20 minutes, or until well risen and a skewer inserted into the middle of the cupcakes comes out clean. Let cool in the pans for 5 minutes before transferring to a wire rack to cool completely.

Put the Meringue Buttercream in a bowl and fold in the strawberry jam. Spread the frosting over the cold cupcakes and arrange the summer berries on top of each one in a lovely cascade. Dust with confectioners' sugar.

These little carved pumpkin-shaped cakes each have their own spooky grin. The selection of Halloween cake sprinkles and paper cupcake cases available in specialty cake decorating shops and online is vast. Look for orange, green, or black paper cases and orange sanding sugar and nonpareils to scatter over the tops and on the serving dish.

jack-o'-lanterns

1 quantity Buttermilk Cake (page 9)

1 quantity Meringue Buttercream (page 11)

black food coloring paste

orange food coloring paste

orange sanding sugar or nonpareils

green jelly beans, for the stalks

Halloween sugar sprinkles (optional), to decorate the serving dish

1–2 muffin pans, lined with orange paper cupcake cases

small piping bag with a small star-shaped tip

makes 12—16

Preheat the oven to 350°F.

Divide the Buttermilk Cake mixture between the paper cupcake cases, filling them two-thirds full, and bake on the middle shelf of the preheated oven for 20 minutes, or until well risen and a skewer inserted into the middle of the cupcakes comes out clean. Let cool in the pans for 5 minutes before transferring to a wire rack to cool completely.

Put the Meringue Buttercream in a bowl. Take out 6 tablespoons and put in a separate bowl. Tint this quantity black (see page 16 for help on tinting) using the black food coloring paste. Color the remaining, large bowl of buttercream orange using the orange food coloring paste.

Spread the orange buttercream over the cold cupcakes, spreading evenly with a palette knife. Using the blunt end of a knife or a wooden skewer, make indents in the buttercream to resemble ridges in the pumpkins. Scatter orange sanding sugar or nonpareils over the buttercream until evenly coated.

Fill the piping bag with the black buttercream. Pipe eyes, a nose, and a mouth onto the orange frosting to make jack-o'-lantern faces. Lay the cupcakes on their side and stick one green jelly bean into the top of each cupcake to make the stalks.

Scatter the serving dish with Halloween sugar sprinkles, if using, and arrange the cupcakes on top to serve.

Whoever would have thought that lurking under these ski caps are cupcakes? These penguins take a little more time to frost than some other recipes, but the cupcakes, caps, beaks, and wings can all be made in advance. Scatter crushed-up meringues over the serving dish to complete the snowy, polar theme.

fat penguins in ski caps

1 quantity Buttermilk Cake (page 9)

1 quantity Vanilla Buttercream (page 12)

black food coloring paste

tiny white chocolate drops

4 oz. white ready-to-roll fondant icing

yellow food coloring paste

red food coloring paste

storebought meringues (optional), to decorate the serving dish

confectioners' sugar, for dusting

muffin pan, lined with 8–10 paper cupcake cases

mini-muffin pan, lined with 8–10 paper cases in the coordinating size

makes 8—10

Preheat the oven to 350°F.

Divide the Buttermilk Cake mixture between the paper cases, filling them two-thirds full, and bake on the middle shelf of the preheated oven for 12–25 minutes. The time will vary according to the size of the cakes—keep an eye on them and take them out when they are well risen and a skewer inserted into the middle of the cakes comes out clean. Let cool in the pans for 5 minutes before transferring to a wire rack to cool completely.

Put two-thirds of the Vanilla Buttercream in a bowl and tint it black (see page 16 for help on tinting) using the black food coloring paste. Leave the rest of the buttercream white.

To make the penguins, remove the paper cases from all the cold cakes and trim the top off each cake to make it level. Lay the larger cupcakes upside down on the clean work surface and dab a little of the buttercream on the top. Lay a mini-muffin upside down on top of each larger cupcake. Using a palette knife, spread black buttercream smoothly all over the penguins, leaving the area for the tummy unfrosted. Spread white buttercream into the tummy area. Press 2 tiny white chocolate drops onto each penguin's face for the eyes. Using a toothpick, dab a little black food coloring onto the middle of each eye.

To make the wings, caps, and beaks, take 1 oz. of the fondant icing and tint it yellow using the food coloring paste. Break off small nuggets of the icing and shape into triangles for the beaks. Stick one onto the front of each penguin. To make the wings, color half of the remaining icing black using the food coloring paste. Pinch off hazelnut-sized pieces and shape and flatten into wings. Press one wing onto either side of each penguin. Use the remaining icing to make the ski caps. Tint three-quarters of it red and leave the remainder white. Roll and pinch the red icing into cone shapes and push the ends so that they droop. Roll the white icing into small balls and prick each one all over with a toothpick to make it look like a pompom. Stick one to the end of each cap. Carefully place a cap on top of each penguin.

Crush the meringues and scatter over a serving dish, lif you like. Dust with confectioners' sugar. Position the penguins around the snow scene.

These wintery chaps have a certain twinkle about them—each one seems to have a slightly different expression. Scatter extra desiccated coconut on the serving dish to make a snowy landscape. The marzipan carrots, eyes, and mouths can be made in advance and stored in an airtight box until ready to use.

snowmen in scarves

2½ oz. natural marzipan

orange food coloring paste

black food coloring paste

1 quantity Buttermilk Cake (page 9)

1 quantity Marshmallow Frosting (page 11)

4 cups desiccated coconut

16–20 red candy-coated chocolate drops

licorice sticks, cut into 8–10 x ½-inch lengths

8–10 large chocolate buttons

muffin pan, lined with 8–10 paper or silver cupcake cases

mini-muffin pan, lined with 8–10 paper or silver cases in the coordinating size

8–10 toothpicks

narrow festive ribbon, cut into 8–10 x 10-inch lengths

makes 8—10

Start making the marzipan noses, mouths, and eyes the day before you make the snowmen. Tint three-quarters of the marzipan orange using the orange food coloring paste (see page 16 for help on tinting). Tint it the shade of orange you like by very gradually adding more coloring. Break off small nuggets of the marzipan and roll between your hands to make carrot shapes.

Tint the remaining marzipan black using the black food coloring paste and roll into tiny balls, allowing roughly 4 for each snowman's mouth and 1 for each eye. Make the balls for the eyes slightly larger than the ones for the mouth. Now let everything dry out overnight on a sheet of baking parchment in an airtight box.

The next day, when you are ready to make the snowmen, preheat the oven to 350°F.

Divide the Buttermilk Cake mixture between the paper cases, filling them two-thirds full, and bake on the middle shelf of the preheated oven for 12–25 minutes. The time will vary according to the size of the cakes—keep an eye on them and take them out when they are well risen and a skewer inserted into the middle of the cakes comes out clean. Let cool in the pans for 5 minutes before transferring to a wire rack to cool completely.

Using a palette knife, spread the Marshmallow Frosting smoothly over the tops of the cold cakes, right to the edges. Before the frosting sets, coat the top of each cake with desiccated coconut. Press the marzipan noses into the middle of each smaller cake and arrange the tiny black marzipan balls as the eyes and mouths. Press the candy-coated chocolate drops down the middle of each larger cupcake to make buttons. To make the hats, dab a tiny amount of frosting in the middle of each chocolate button and stick the licorice onto it.

Lay each large cupcake on its side with the coconut facing you and the buttons in a vertical line. Carefully push a toothpick into what is now the top of each cake so that there is still ¾ inch of the stick exposed. Push a mini-muffin onto the toothpick to make the head. Tie a length of ribbon around the neck of each snowman and balance the hat on top of his head.

Scatter desiccated coconut over a serving dish and position the snowmen on it.

These cupcakes would be perfect for a wedding or sophisticated bachelorette party. The letters are made from royal icing and should be finished at least 48 hours before serving to allow them time to harden. They will keep for up to a week, so you can make them well in advance. They can also be tinted using food coloring pastes according to your color scheme, or sprinkled with glitter, as we've done here.

signature cupcakes

1 quantity Royal Icing (page 13)

edible glitter in a color of your choice

1 quantity Buttermilk Cake (page 9)

1 quantity Marshmallow Frosting (page 11)

small piping bag with a small star-shaped tip

baking sheet, lined with baking parchment

1–2 muffin pans, lined with silver paper cupcake cases

small piping bag with a large star-shaped tip

makes 12—16

Start making the royal-icing letters 2 days before you make the cupcakes. Make sure the Royal Icing is stiff-peak consistency—i.e. stiff enough to hold its shape once piped—so add more confectioners' sugar if you need to.

See opposite for instructions on how to make the letters.

When you are ready to make the cupcakes, preheat the oven to 350°F.

Divide the Buttermilk Cake mixture between the paper cupcake cases, filling them two-thirds full, and bake on the middle shelf of the preheated oven for 20 minutes, or until well risen and a skewer inserted into the middle of the cupcakes comes out clean. Let cool in the pans for 5 minutes before transferring to a wire rack to cool completely.

Fill the piping bag with the large star-shaped tip with the Marshmallow Frosting. Pipe generous swirls over each cold cupcake and sprinkle with edible glitter. Allow to set for about 30 minutes.

Very carefully peel the set royal-icing letters off the baking parchment and arrange on top of each cupcake, pushing them gently into the frosting.

1

2

how to make
royal-icing letters

※ Fill the piping bag with the small star-shaped tip with the Royal Icing.

※ Put the baking sheet lined with baking parchment in front of you on the work surface.

※ Pipe the required letters onto the baking parchment. Take it slowly until you get used to making the letters and make sure that separate strokes within a letter are well attached so that they don't break off when you stand them up later. **(1)**

※ While the icing is still wet, sprinkle with edible glitter. **(2)**

※ Make more letters than you require to allow for breakages.

※ Set aside to dry for at least 48 hours.

I found these mini terracotta pots in my garden center and they are the perfect scale to serve these cupcakes in, but you can leave them out of the recipe if you can't find them. Piping flowers in buttercream is really quite simple, but practice makes perfect. If at first you're not happy with your flowers, simply scrape the buttercream off the top of the cakes and start again. You can buy tips especially for making petals—they are curved and usually called petal or leaf tips—but do experiment with different shapes to find the most effective ones.

little flower pots

1 quantity Buttermilk Cake (page 9)

1 quantity Meringue Buttercream (page 11)

assorted food coloring pastes

tiny sugar flowers

muffin pan, lined with 8–10 paper cupcake cases

mini-muffin pan, lined with 8–10 paper cases in the coordinating size

mini terracotta pots in 2 sizes

piping bags fitted with assorted petal tips (see page 14 for some of the tips available)

makes about 16

Preheat the oven to 350°F.

Divide the Buttermilk Cake mixture between the cupcake cases, filling them two-thirds full, and bake on the middle shelf of the preheated oven for 12–25 minutes. The time will vary according to the size of the cakes—keep an eye on them and take them out when they are well risen and a skewer inserted into the middle of the cakes comes out clean. Let cool in the pans for 5 minutes before transferring to a wire rack to cool completely.

Divide the Meringue Buttercream between however many bowls you need for the colors you're using and tint each one a different color (see page 16 for help on tinting) using the food coloring pastes. Tint them the shade you like by very gradually adding more coloring.

Cover the top of each cold cupcake with buttercream, spreading evenly with a palette knife. Fit the piping bag with your chosen tip and fill with buttercream. Holding the bag at a 45-degree angle to the cake, pipe petal shapes over the top of the cakes. Finish off each cake with a tiny sugar flower in the center.

Carefully place one cake in each terracotta pot to serve.

1 quantity Double Chocolate or
Buttermilk Cake (page 9)

1 quantity Marshmallow
Frosting (page 11)

1 quantity Chocolate Glaze
(page 12)

jimmies

*1–2 muffin pans, lined with
paper cupcake cases*

*large piping bag with a plain
½-inch tip*

makes 12—16

**A rich, bittersweet chocolate cupcake topped with a mound of luscious
marshmallowy frosting and coated in a glossy chocolate glaze. Does a
cupcake get any better than this?**

hi-hat cupcakes

Preheat the oven to 350°F.

Divide the Double Chocolate or Buttermilk Cake mixture between the paper cupcake
cases, filling them two-thirds full, and bake on the middle shelf of the preheated
oven for 20 minutes, or until well risen and a skewer inserted into the middle of the
cupcakes comes out clean. Let cool in the pans for 5 minutes before transferring to
a wire rack to cool completely.

See opposite for instructions on how to decorate the cupcakes.

how to decorate
hi-hat cupcakes

✳ Fill the piping bag with the Marshmallow Frosting.

✳ Pipe the frosting into a cone shape on top of each cold cupcake. Don't pipe the frosting right to the edge of the cupcake—leave a thin border between the frosting and the top of the paper case. **(1)**

✳ Let the frosting set for at least 30 minutes before coating in the Chocolate Glaze.

✳ When you've made the Chocolate Glaze, let it cool slightly before using. Make sure it's in a small but deep bowl, so that when you dip the cupcake hats in, they fit in without getting squashed.

✳ Holding the cupcake upside down, submerge the frosting in the glaze. Allow any excess glaze to drip back into the bowl. The frosting should be completely covered in chocolate glaze. **(2)**

✳ Allow to set for 5 minutes.

✳ Finally, scatter the jimmies over the top and leave until completely set.

These brownies are strictly for adults! They are rich, dark, sticky, very chocolatey, and loaded with dried cherries and hazelnuts. They are just as good served plain without the frosting and with a scoop of luxury vanilla or chocolate ice cream. Make the chocolate and glass hearts in advance and store in a cool, dry place until ready to serve.

double chocolate, hazelnut, and dried cherry brownie squares

1 cup skinned hazelnuts

8 oz. chocolate, chopped

10 tablespoons unsalted butter

1½ cups packed light brown sugar or light muscovado

4 eggs

1 teaspoon pure vanilla extract

1 cup all-purpose flour

a pinch of salt

1 cup dried cherries

to decorate

½ quantity Chocolate Fudge Frosting (page 12)

1 bag fruit-flavored hard candies

4½ oz. bittersweet chocolate, chopped

pink and/or red sprinkles

9-inch square baking pan, greased and baselined with baking parchment

assorted heart-shaped cutters, oiled

2 solid baking sheets, lined with baking parchment

makes about 16

Preheat the oven to 350°F.

Put the hazelnuts on a baking sheet and toast in the preheated oven for 5 minutes. Let cool slightly, then roughly chop and set aside. Leave the oven on.

Put the chocolate and butter in a heatproof bowl set over a pan of barely simmering water. Stir until smooth and thoroughly combined. Let cool slightly.

Put the eggs and sugar in the bowl of a freestanding electric mixer fitted with the whisk attachment (or use an electric whisk and mixing bowl) and beat until pale and light. Add the vanilla and chocolate mixture and mix until combined. Sift the flour and salt and fold into the mixture with the chopped hazelnuts and cherries.

Pour the mixture into the prepared baking pan and bake on the middle shelf of the hot oven for 25 minutes. Let cool in the pan until completely cold.

Spread the Chocolate Fudge Frosting over the cold brownie and allow to set before cutting into squares. Now see overleaf for instructions on how to make the hearts.

Arrange the "glass" and speckled chocolate hearts on top of the brownie squares just before serving, as they can melt if left sitting in the frosting for too long.

1

2

how to make
"glass" hearts

✳ Divide the hard candies into separate colors and pop into plastic food bags. Just use red ones for these hearts, if you like. Using a rolling pin or mortar and pestle, crush the candies into small pieces. **(1)**

✳ Preheat the oven to 325°F, if possible on the conventional setting, not using the convection.

✳ Arrange the well-oiled heart-shaped cutters on one of the prepared baking sheets. Make the hearts in small quantities, as you will need to work quickly once they come out of the oven.

✳ Carefully fill the cutters with the crushed candies in an even, thin layer. **(2)**

✳ Bake on the middle shelf of the preheated oven for about 5 minutes, or until melted and smooth. You will need to keep a close eye on the timing, as it can vary depending on the size of cutters and the quantity of candies used.

✳ Once the candies have melted and filled the cutters, remove from the oven and let cool and harden for a couple of minutes. Very carefully push the "glass" hearts from the cutters.

✳ Repeat with different colors as desired.

✳ The "glass" hearts will keep for 24 hours in a cool, dry place.

3

4

how to make
speckled chocolate hearts

✳ Put the chocolate in a heatproof bowl set over a pan of barely simmering water. Stir until smooth and melted.

✳ Pour the melted chocolate onto the second prepared baking sheet. Spread into a thin layer using a palette knife and set aside to cool for 5 minutes. **(3)**

✳ Scatter with pink and/or red sprinkles and leave until completely set and firm. **(4)**

✳ Using a heart-shaped cutter, carefully stamp out shapes from the chocolate. **(5)** Store either in a cool place or in the refrigerator until required.

5

Make the cake base the day before you plan to frost these cakes—this makes the fondant fancies easier to cut and frost. These little cakes are enough for just a couple of mouthfuls and look beautiful frosted in contrasting delicate colors.

fondant fancies

10 tablespoons unsalted butter, softened

¾ cup sugar

2 eggs, beaten

1 cup plus 2 tablespoons all-purpose flour

2 teaspoons baking powder

3–4 tablespoons milk, at room temperature

⅓ cup ground almonds

finely grated zest and freshly squeezed juice of ½ unwaxed lemon

2 tablespoons jarred lemon curd

to decorate

1 tablespoon sieved apricot jam, warmed

confectioners' sugar, for dusting

3½ oz. natural marzipan

1 lb. fondant icing sugar

freshly squeezed juice of 1 lemon

pink food coloring paste

yellow food coloring paste

blue food coloring paste

1 cup royal icing sugar

tiny sugar flowers

8-inch square baking pan, greased and baselined with baking parchment

small piping bag with a fine writing tip, or make your own (see page 15)

makes 12—16

The day before you want to serve the fondant fancies, preheat the oven to 350°F.

Cream together the butter and sugar until light and creamy in the bowl of a freestanding mixer (or use an electric whisk and mixing bowl). Gradually add the beaten eggs, mixing well between each addition and scraping down the side of the mixing bowl from time to time.

Sift together the flour and baking powder and add to the mixture in alternate batches with the milk. Fold in the ground almonds, lemon zest and juice and stir until smooth.

Spoon the batter into the prepared baking pan. Spread level and bake on the middle shelf of the preheated oven for about 25 minutes, or until a skewer inserted into the middle of the cake comes out clean. Remove from the oven and let cool in the pan for 5–10 minutes before turning out onto a wire rack to cool completely.

The next day, split the cake in half horizontally using a long, serrated knife. Spread the lemon curd over the bottom layer and sandwich the 2 layers back together. Brush the warmed apricot jam over the top of the cake. Lightly dust a work surface with confectioners' sugar. Roll out the marzipan to a square the same size as the top of the cake, using the baking pan as a guide. Lay the marzipan on top of the jam and smooth the surface. Trim the sides of the cake and cut into neat, 1½-inch cubes.

Mix the fondant icing sugar with enough lemon juice to make a smooth, thick icing suitable to coat the cakes. Divide the icing between 3 bowls and tint each one pink, yellow, or blue (see page 16 for help on tinting) using the food coloring pastes. Tint them the shade you like by very gradually adding more coloring. Cover 2 of the bowls with plastic wrap while you work with the third. Coat the top and sides of each cake with this color of icing. The easiest way to do this is to hold one cake on a fork over the bowl and drizzle the icing over the top and sides to coat evenly. Transfer the cakes to a wire rack and leave for at least 1 hour, or until set. Continue with the other colors of icing until you have coated all the cakes.

Whisk together the royal icing sugar and a little water until it is thick enough to pipe. Spoon into the piping bag and use to pipe thin lines and dots over the top of each cake. Decorate with tiny sugar flowers. Allow to set before serving.

large cakes

This is the perfect cake for a celebration such as a wedding or christening. It's dark, dense, and very rich. It would be delicious to serve as a dessert with a compote of summer berries and lightly whipped heavy cream. As the cake is very moist, it can be made a couple of days before frosting and serving. It can also be frozen frosted, wrapped well in plastic wrap. Defrost completely before frosting.

rich chocolate celebration cake

10 oz. bittersweet chocolate (at least 70% cocoa solids), chopped

14 tablespoons unsalted butter

6 eggs, separated

1 cup sugar

1 cup ground almonds

½ teaspoon cream of tartar

a pinch of salt

frosting

¼ cup tablespoons sieved apricot jam, warmed

confectioners' sugar, for dusting

8 oz. natural marzipan

1 quantity Chocolate Ganache (page 12)

roses

12 oz. white sugar paste

pink food coloring paste

9-inch springform cake pan, greased, lightly floured and baselined with baking parchment

serves 12—16

Preheat the oven to 350°F.

Put the chocolate and butter in a heatproof bowl set over a pan of barely simmering water. Stir until smooth and thoroughly combined. Let cool slightly.

Put the egg yolks and sugar in the bowl of a freestanding mixer fitted with the whisk attachment (or use an electric whisk and mixing bowl) and beat until pale and very thick. Stir in the chocolate mixture. Add the ground almonds and mix well.

Put the egg whites, cream of tartar, and salt in a grease-free bowl and whisk until they just form stiff peaks. Fold a large spoonful of the egg whites into the chocolate mixture to loosen, then carefully fold in the remainder.

Spoon the mixture into the prepared cake pan and bake on the middle shelf of the preheated oven for about 1 hour, or until the cake has formed a crust and a skewer inserted into the middle of the cake comes out with a moist crumb. Remove from the oven and let cool in the pan.

Once the cake is completely cold (or the next day), it can be frosted.

Place the cake on a wire rack set over a baking sheet. If the top of the cake is uneven, you may need to slice it off to make a flat surface. Brush the top and side of the cake with some of the warmed apricot jam. Lightly dust a clean, dry work surface with confectioners' sugar and roll the marzipan out into a large, thin round big enough to cover the whole cake. Lay the marzipan on top of the jam and smooth the surface. Trim the excess, then brush with a little more apricot jam.

Pour the slightly cooled and thickened Chocolate Ganache over the top of the cake and use a palette knife to smooth the top and side. Leave the cake in a cool place to allow the ganache to set.

Now see overleaf for instructions on how to make the roses.

Arrange the dried sugar-paste roses on the cake.

1

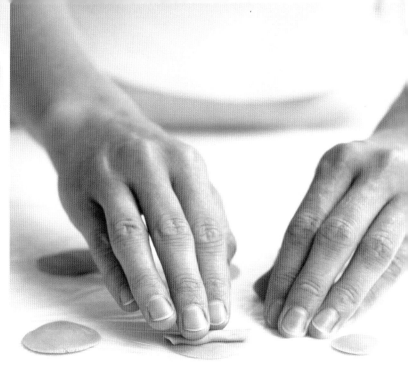

2

3

4

how to make
sugar-paste roses

✳ Tint the sugar paste different shades of pink (see page 16 for help on tinting) using the pink food coloring paste, very gradually adding more coloring for a stronger color.

✳ Lay a large sheet of plastic wrap on the work surface. Break off small nuggets of the sugar paste and roll between your hands to make little balls of different sizes. Place on the plastic wrap.

✳ Cover with more plastic wrap. Using your thumb, flatten each ball until quite thin. It doesn't matter if they're irregular disks. **(1)**

✳ Peel off the top layer of plastic wrap. Start with a small disk of sugar paste and, using your fingers, gently roll the disk into a spiral to form the center of the rose. **(2)**

✳ Take another petal and carefully wrap this around the central one, covering the seam. **(3)**

✳ As you add the petals, gently squeeze the edges to make them more shapely and curved. Continue until you have created a rose in the size you require. **(4)**

✳ Pinch off any excess sugar paste from under the rose and stand it upright on baking parchment. Continue until you have the required number of roses, then let them dry for 2 days.

I like to serve this pretty cake for Mother's Day or when I have a girly gathering. Choose rose petals in two different shapes of pink and crystallize them as described on page 66. The cake can be baked and the fresh coconut shavings toasted a day in advance.

pistachio, coconut, and lime cake

1¼ cups shelled, unsalted pistachio nuts

½ cup desiccated coconut

finely grated zest of 2 limes and freshly squeezed juice of 1

1 cup all-purpose flour

2 teaspoons baking powder

a pinch of salt

15 tablespoons unsalted butter, softened

1 cup sugar

4 eggs, beaten

1 teaspoon rosewater

to decorate

½ fresh coconut

finely grated zest and freshly squeezed juice of 2 limes

1½–2 cups confectioners' sugar, sifted

⅓ cup shelled, unsalted pistachio nuts, chopped

pink rose petals, crystallized (page 66)

9-inch ring cake mold, greased and lightly floured

baking sheet, lined with baking parchment

serves 6—8

Preheat the oven to 350°F.

Put the pistachio nuts in a food processor and pulse until finely chopped. Mix with the desiccated coconut and lime zest. In a separate bowl, sift together the flour, baking powder, and salt.

Cream together the butter and sugar until light and creamy in the bowl of a freestanding mixer (or use an electric whisk and mixing bowl). Gradually add the beaten eggs, mixing well between each addition and scraping down the side of the mixing bowl from time to time. Add the rosewater and mix again.

Add the pistachio nuts, coconut, and lime zest and mix until smooth. Add the sifted dry ingredients and mix again. Finally, add the lime juice and beat until smooth.

Pour the mixture into the prepared cake mold, spread level, and bake on the middle shelf of the preheated oven for about 35–40 minutes, or until a skewer inserted into the middle of the cake comes out clean. Let cool in the mold for 5 minutes, then carefully turn out onto a wire rack to cool completely. Leave the oven on.

To decorate, crack open the coconut and remove the flesh. Using a vegetable peeler, shave the flesh into strips. Arrange the strips in a single layer on the prepared baking sheet and toast in the hot oven for about 10 minutes, or until lightly golden. Keep an eye on it, as it can easily burn.

Put the lime zest, juice, and confectioners' sugar in a bowl and beat until smooth and the right consistency to just drip over the edges of the cake. You may need a little more or less confectioners' sugar depending on how juicy the limes are.

Place the cake on a serving plate and, using a spoon, carefully cover the top of the cake with the frosting, allowing some to dip over the sides. Allow to set.

Scatter the cooled, toasted coconut shavings, chopped pistachio nuts, and crystallized rose petals all over the frosted cake and serve.

I have decorated this cake with small sugar-paste flowers. These are so easy to make—just follow the instructions on page 125 (and allow to dry out for 2 days) or look out for ready-made ones in sugarcraft stores. If you prefer, you could always decorate your teapot with a selection of candy. For the teapot, you'll need to make the recipe below twice so that you have 2 identical cake pieces for the finished pot.

tea for two

for half of the teapot

11 tablespoons unsalted butter, softened

¾ cup plus 2 tablespoons sugar

3 eggs, beaten

1 teaspoon pure vanilla extract

1½ cups all-purpose flour

3 teaspoons baking powder

3 tablespoons milk, at room temperature

to decorate

confectioners' sugar, for dusting

5 oz. white sugar paste

lilac food coloring paste

blue coloring paste

1 quantity Marshmallow Frosting (page 11)

¼ cup sieved apricot jam, warmed

a little Royal Icing (page 13) (optional)

yellow food coloring paste (optional)

3 sticks of dowel

assorted small flower-shaped cutters

small piping bag with a fine writing tip, or make your own (see page 15)

1-quart ovenproof Pyrex bowl, greased and lightly floured

serves 8

Make the teapot handle and spout at least 2 days before you make the cake. Lightly dust a clean, dry work surface with confectioners' sugar. Take 1½ oz. of the sugar paste and roll to make a sausage shape with one end slightly thicker than the other. Bend into a spout shape. Take another 1½ oz. of the sugar paste and roll to make a sausage. Bend into a handle shape. Push a length of dowel into both ends of the handle and the thicker end of the spout so that they stick out by at least 1½ inches.

Turn to page 125 to make sugar-paste flowers with the remaining sugar paste. At the same time, make a small ball to go on top of the teapot lid. Leave both the flowers, teapot handle, and spout to dry out completely on baking parchment for at least 2 days before using.

When you are ready to make the cake, preheat the oven to 350°F and position the shelf in the bottom third of the oven.

Cream together the butter and sugar until light and creamy in the bowl of a freestanding mixer (or use an electric whisk and mixing bowl). Gradually add the beaten eggs, mixing well between each addition and scraping down the side of the mixing bowl from time to time. Add the vanilla.

Sift together the flour and baking powder. Add to the cake mixture along with the milk and mix until smooth.

Spoon the mixture into the prepared Pyrex bowl and spread level with a palette knife. Bake in the preheated oven for about 45 minutes, or until a skewer inserted in the middle of the cake comes out clean. Let cool in the bowl for 5 minutes before turning out onto a wire rack to cool completely.

Repeat as above for the second half of the teapot.

Now refer to the step instructions overleaf for assembling the cake.

how to assemble
a teapot cake

✳ Place one cake, rounded side down, on a serving plate. Using a palette knife, cover the flat side with Marshmallow Frosting. **(1)**

✳ Lay the second cake, rounded side up, on top of this cake. Brush the apricot jam all over the cake. Cover the whole cake with marshmallow frosting, spreading smoothly with a palette knife. **(2)**

✳ Get the spout, handle, and sugar-paste flowers ready. **(3)**

✳ Before the frosting sets, arrange the flowers over the teapot, pressing them onto the frosting. Top with the ball for the lid. **(4)**

✳ Push the handle and spout into either side of the cake, allowing the bottom of the handle to rest on the serving plate.

✳ If you like, you can finish off the flowers with a dot of yellow-tinted royal icing in the centers.

To get ahead, make the cake base and the cookie dough for this fabulous creation the day before you plan to serve it.

dog house

2 sticks unsalted butter, softened

1¼ cups sugar

4 eggs, beaten

1 teaspoon pure vanilla extract

2 cups all-purpose flour

4 teaspoons baking powder

3–4 tablespoons milk, at room temperature

1 quantity Vanilla Buttercream (page 12)

6½ oz. milk chocolate, for the chocolate panels

1½ oz. white chocolate

7–8 oz. milk chocolate buttons

2 oz. white chocolate chips

dogs

1 quantity Gingerbread Cookies (page 10)

all-purpose flour, for dusting

1 quantity Royal Icing (page 13)

assorted food coloring pastes, to match your breeds of dog!

9 x 13-inch baking pan, lined with baking parchment and greased

assorted dog-shaped cookie cutters

2 baking sheets, lined with baking parchment

small piping bag with a fine writing tip, or make your own (see page 15)

serves 8—10

Preheat the oven to 350°F.

Cream together the butter and sugar until light and creamy. Gradually add the beaten eggs, mixing well between each addition and scraping down the side of the mixing bowl from time to time. Add the vanilla. Sift together the flour and baking powder and add to the mixture in 2 batches. Stir in the milk. Mix until smooth, then spoon into the prepared baking pan and spread level with a palette knife. Bake on the middle shelf of the preheated oven for 35–40 minutes, or until a skewer inserted into the middle of the cake comes out clean. Let cool in the pan for 5 minutes before turning out onto a wire rack to cool completely. Once cold, wrap in plastic wrap until you are ready to assemble the dog house. Leave the oven on.

Take the Gingerbread Cookie dough out of the refrigerator and put it on a lightly floured work surface. Roll it out to a thickness of ⅛ inch. Using the cookie cutters, carefully stamp out dog shapes. Arrange them on the prepared baking sheets. Gather together the scraps of the dough and re-roll to make more shapes. Bake on the middle shelf of the preheated oven for 10–12 minutes, or until firm and the edges are just starting to brown, swapping the sheets around if needed. Let cool on the sheets for about 5 minutes before transferring to a wire rack to cool completely.

Divide the Royal Icing between however many bowls you need for the colors you're using and tint each one a different color (see page 16 for help on tinting) using the food coloring pastes. Fill the piping bag with whichever color you want to start with. Pipe borders around the cold cookies. "Flood" the area inside the borders with icing (see page 44 for step pictures of "flooding"), spreading it carefully up to the edges with a mini palette knife or small knife. Let it dry and harden slightly, then decorate or accessorize as you like!

When you are ready to assemble the cake, cut it into quarters and place one quarter on a serving platter. Cover the top with 2 tablespoons of the Vanilla Buttercream, spreading evenly with a palette knife. Repeat so that you have 4 layers of cake and 3 layers of buttercream. Using a long, sharp knife, cut into the long sides to make a roof shape. Cover the whole cake with buttercream and leave somewhere cool.

Make the chocolate panels as described on page 121. At the same time, make a door shape out of the white chocolate. Cut the panels to fit the walls of the dog house (vertically for the short sides and horizontally for the long). Stick them to the buttercream. Attach the door with a little buttercream. Tile the roof with the chocolate buttons and chips. Arrange the dogs in front of the house and serve.

This is really a grown-up English Victoria Sponge with a few added extras. The meringue buttercream gets an extra hit of vanilla with the addition of the seeds from a vanilla bean. Try to use small, extra-sweet berries—wild strawberries are particularly pretty—and the best possible strawberry jam you can find. If you were to use homemade jam, that would take this cake all the way to the top.

high summer cake

15 tablespoons unsalted butter, softened

1½ cups sugar

4 eggs, beaten

2 teaspoons pure vanilla extract

finely grated zest of 1 unwaxed lemon

2 cups all-purpose flour

2 teaspoons baking powder

1 teaspoon baking soda

a pinch of salt

¾ cup buttermilk

6 tablespoons strawberry jam

1 quantity Meringue Buttercream (page 11, but using seeds scraped out of a vanilla bean in place of the vanilla extract)

6½ oz. white chocolate, coarsely grated

2½ cups small strawberries and/or wild strawberries (if possible)

1½ cups raspberries

1 cup red currants, crystallized (page 66)

2 x 8-inch round cake pans, greased and baselined with baking parchment

serves 8

Preheat the oven to 350°F.

Cream together the butter and sugar until light and creamy in the bowl of a freestanding mixer (or use an electric whisk and mixing bowl). Gradually add the beaten eggs, mixing well between each addition and scraping down the side of the mixing bowl from time to time. Add the vanilla and lemon zest and mix again.

Sift together the flour, baking powder, baking soda, and salt. Add to the cake mixture with the buttermilk and mix again until smooth.

Divide the mixture between the prepared cake pans and bake on the middle shelf of the preheated oven for about 35 minutes, or until well risen, golden, and a skewer inserted into the middle of the cakes comes out clean. Let cool in the pans for 5 minutes, then transfer to a wire rack to cool completely.

Cut the cold cakes in half horizontally, using a long, serrated knife. Place one layer on a serving plate and spread with 2 tablespoons of the strawberry jam. Spread 2 tablespoons of the Meringue Buttercream over the jam and top with another cake layer. Repeat with the remaining cake layers, leaving the top layer plain. Gently press the cake layers together. Cover the side of the cake with buttercream, spreading evenly with a palette knife.

Scatter the grated white chocolate onto a tray and, holding the cake very carefully in both hands, roll the side in the grated chocolate to coat completely. Spread a thick layer of buttercream on top of the cake and finish with the mixed berries and crystallized red currants. Serve immediately.

This cake looks wildly impressive, but is actually quite easy to make and assemble. You just need to allow plenty of time and patience—it's not one to be knocked up in an afternoon. Make the cake layers the day before you plan to serve the finished cake.

dark and white chocolate layer cake

4 oz. bittersweet chocolate, chopped

2⅓ cups all-purpose flour

2 teaspoons baking soda

a pinch of salt

1 stick unsalted butter, softened

2 cups packed light brown sugar

4 eggs, beaten

1 teaspoon pure vanilla extract

1 cup sour cream

1 cup boiling water

1 quantity Chocolate Meringue Buttercream (page 11)

ganache

1 cup heavy cream

2 tablespoons unsalted butter

2 tablespoons sugar

6½ oz. bittersweet chocolate, finely chopped

1 teaspoon coffee essence

chocolate panels

6½ oz. bittersweet chocolate, chopped

6½ oz. white chocolate, chopped

2 x 8-inch square cake pans, greased, baselined with baking parchment, and greased

2 piping bags with star-shaped tips

baking sheet, lined with baking parchment

serves 16

Preheat the oven to 350°F.

Put the chocolate for the cake in a heatproof bowl set over a pan of barely simmering water. Stir until smooth and melted. Let cool slightly.

Sift the flour, baking soda, and salt into a bowl.

Cream together the butter and sugar until light and creamy. Gradually add the beaten eggs, mixing well between each addition and scraping down the side of the mixing bowl from time to time. Add the vanilla and melted chocolate and mix. Mix in one-third of the sifted dry ingredients, followed by half the sour cream. Repeat and finish with the remaining third of the sifted dry ingredients. Now add the boiling water, mixing well to ensure everything is thoroughly combined.

Divide the mixture between the prepared cake pans, spread level, and bake on the middle shelf of the preheated oven for about 30–35 minutes, or until a skewer inserted into the middle of the cakes comes out clean. Let cool in the pans for 5–10 minutes, then turn out onto a wire rack to cool completely. If you are not assembling the cakes straightaway, wrap in plastic wrap until needed.

To make the ganache, put the cream, butter, and sugar in a small saucepan and heat until just boiling. Pour over the chopped chocolate and let melt for 5 minutes. Add the coffee essence, stir to combine, then set aside.

When you are ready to assemble the cake, cut the cold cakes in half horizontally, using a long, serrated knife. Place one layer on a serving plate and spread with 3–4 tablespoons of the Chocolate Meringue Buttercream. Top with a second cake layer and spread with 3–4 tablespoons of ganache. Top with a third cake layer and spread with more buttercream. Top with the last cake layer. Gently press the layers together. Now spread buttercream evenly all over the top and side of the cake.

Fill one piping bag with the remaining buttercream and the other with the remaining ganache. Pipe rosettes in straight lines across the top of the cake, alternating between buttercream and ganache.

Now see opposite for instructions on how to make the chocolate panels.

Arrange the bittersweet and white chocolate panels alternately around the outside of the cake, pressing them into the buttercream to stick.

1

2

how to make
chocolate panels

✳ Put the bittersweet chocolate in a heatproof bowl set over a pan of barely simmering water. Stir until thoroughly smooth and melted.

✳ Pour the melted chocolate onto the prepared baking sheet. Spread into a thin layer using a palette knife and set aside until completely set.

✳ Using a large, sharp knife, trim the edges of the chocolate to make an even rectangle. Cut into strips about 1 inch wide. **(1)**

✳ Trim the strips so that they are just a little taller than the frosted cake. **(2)**

✳ Repeat the steps above with the white chocolate.

I've made the flowers here in a variety of colors to match the butterflies hovering above the cake. Hat-making suppliers or craft stores are a good source for the ribbon and butterflies. Make the beautiful sugar-paste flowers 2 days in advance to allow them time to dry out.

blossom cake

1 quantity Buttermilk Cake (page 9)

6 tablespoons jarred lemon curd

3 tablespoons mascarpone

3 tablespoons sieved apricot jam, warmed

to decorate

8 oz. white sugar paste

yellow food coloring paste

orange food coloring paste

pink food coloring paste

red food coloring paste

1 lb. natural marzipan

1 lb. white ready-to-roll fondant icing

2–3 tablespoons confectioners' sugar, plus extra for dusting

assorted small flower-shaped cutters

embossing tools (optional)

2 x 8-inch round cake pans, greased, baselined with baking parchment, and greased

small piping bag with a fine writing tip, or make your own (see page 15)

feather butterflies (optional)

white craft wire

wide ribbon to match your color scheme

serves 8

See overleaf for step instructions on how to make sugar-paste flowers. Allow to dry out for 2 days before you make the cake.

When you are ready to make the cake, preheat the oven to 350°F.

Divide the Buttermilk Cake mixture between the prepared cake pans, spread level, and bake on the middle shelf of the preheated oven for about 25 minutes, or until a skewer inserted into the middle of the cakes comes out clean. You may need to turn the pans halfway through cooking. Let cool in the pans for 5 minutes before turning out onto a wire rack to cool completely.

Cut the cold cakes in half horizontally, using a long, serrated knife. Place one layer on a serving plate and spread with half the lemon curd. Cover with another cake layer and spread this with the mascarpone. Top with a third cake layer and spread with the remaining lemon curd. Top with the last cake layer. Gently press the layers together. Brush the warmed apricot jam all over the cake.

Lightly dust a work surface with confectioners' sugar. Roll out the marzipan to a thickness of ⅛ inch. Using a rolling pin, carefully transfer the marzipan to the cake and drape it on top to cover completely. Using your hands, smooth the marzipan over the top and side and trim off any excess. Brush with a little boiled water.

Roll out the fondant icing and cover the cake with it in the same way as you did with the marzipan. Set aside to dry for a couple of hours.

In a small bowl, mix the confectioners' sugar with a tiny amount of water to make a paste. Fill the piping bag with this icing and pipe small dots on the underside of each sugar-paste flower. Stick them around the side and on top of the cake. Stick the tiny sugar-paste balls to the centers of the flowers with a dot of icing.

Attach the feather butterflies to wires, if using, and push into the cake so that they hover delicately above the blossoms. Finally, wrap a coordinating ribbon around the bottom of the cake and secure with a small dot of icing.

how to make
sugar-paste flowers

✳ Tint the sugar paste yellow, orange, pink, and red (see page 16 for help on tinting) using the food coloring pastes. Tint them the shades you like by very gradually adding more coloring.

✳ Lightly dust a clean, dry work surface with confectioners' sugar. Roll the sugar paste out to a thickness of ⅟₁₆ inch. Chop off tiny pieces and roll into balls for the centers of the flowers.

✳ Using the assorted flower-shaped cutters, stamp out flowers in a variety of shapes and sizes. Create details on the flowers with embossing tools or a wooden skewer.

✳ Press the flowers over the backs of spoons to create more interesting shapes while they set. Allow them to dry out for 2 days.

suppliers and stockists

Confectionery House
www.confectioneryhouse.com
Tel: 518 279 4250
Stockists of paper cases in every color and size, for every occasion, as well as sprinkles and edible decorations

Cool Cupcakes
www.coolcupcakes.com
Tel: 1 800 797 2887
Baking enthusiasts and the cupcake-obsessed will find sanding sugar, edible glitter and sprinkles in a rainbow of colors, plus paper cases and three-, four-, five-, and six-tier cupcake stands on this comprehensive website.

Crate & Barrel
www.crateandbarrel.com
Tel: 800 967 6696
Store and online supplier of kitchenware, such as muffin pans, silicone bakeware, seasonal paper cases, candy thermometers, and cupcake carriers.

H. O. Foose Tinsmithing
www.foosecookiecutters.com
US-based supplier with an incredible selection of more than 700 hand-made cookie cutters. If you can't find what you're looking for on this site you can buy kits to make up your own designs. They also do lots of miniature cutters which are useful for sugar-paste and fondant-icing shapes.

Karen's Cookies
www.karenscookies.net
Tel: 1 800 934 3997
For high-heeled shoes, different breeds of dog, critters big and small, and flowers of all shapes, you'll find the cookie cutter you need at Karen's Cookies. An excellent source for edible sprinkles in every shape and color.

Kitchen Krafts
www.kitchenkrafts.com
Tel: 800 298 5389
Lots and lots of bakeware, candy, cake decorating tools and ready-made icings, cookie cutters, piping bags and tips, and even cupcake pedestals!

Paper Orchid
www.paperorchidstationery.com
Tel: 1 866 280 2125
Supplier of beautiful laser-cut cupcake and cake wrappers.

Pottery Barn
www.potterybarn.com
Tel: 1 888 779 5176
Beautiful selection of cake stands, from the simplest designs, to tiered and elegant miniature examples.

Sugarcraft
www.sugarcraft.com
Every type of cake decoration imaginable, plus useful boxes for presenting and carrying cupcakes, cakes, and cookies as gifts.

Sur la Table
www.surlatable.com
Tel: 800 243 0852
Check online for details of your nearest store. Offers a full line of cookie and cupcake bakeware including cupcake cookie cutters, muffin pans, and piping bags and tips. A good source for specialty ingredients too, such as ready-to-use fondant and fondant and icing sugar. More than 70 retail stores nationwide and an extensive online site.

Williams-Sonoma
www.williams-sonoma.com
Tel: 1 877 812 6235
Cupcake and muffin pans, cake stands, and more.

Wilton
www.wilton.com
The site to browse for all manner of baking and decorating supplies. Packed with patterned and themed paper cases, sprinkles, food coloring, and decorations to suit every possible occasion and theme.

The publisher would like to thank **KitchenAid** for the loan of the stand mixer featured in this book. Visit **www.kitchenaid.com** for more of their products and your nearest stockist.

index

conversion chart

Volume equivalents:

American	Metric	Imperial
6 tbsp butter	85 g	3 oz.
7 tbsp butter	100 g	3½ oz.
1 stick butter	115 g	4 oz.
1 teaspoon	5 ml	
1 tablespoon	15 ml	
¼ cup	60 ml	2 fl.oz.
⅓ cup	75 ml	2½ fl.oz.
½ cup	125 ml	4 fl.oz.
⅔ cup	150 ml	5 fl.oz. (¼ pint)
¾ cup	175 ml	6 fl.oz.
1 cup	250 ml	8 fl.oz.

Oven temperatures:

120°C/130°C	(250°F)	Gas ½
140°C	(275°F)	Gas 1
150°C	(300°F)	Gas 2
160°C/170°C	(325°F)	Gas 3
180°C	(350°F)	Gas 4
190°C	(375°F)	Gas 5
200°C	(400°F)	Gas 6
220°C	(425°F)	Gas 7

Weight equivalents:

Imperial	Metric
1 oz.	30 g
2 oz.	55 g
3 oz.	85 g
3½ oz.	100 g
4 oz.	115 g
5 oz.	140 g
6 oz.	175 g
8 oz. (½ lb.)	225 g
9 oz.	250 g
10 oz.	280 g
11½ oz.	325 g
12 oz.	350 g
13 oz.	375 g
14 oz.	400 g
15 oz.	425 g
16 oz. (1 lb.)	450 g

Measurements:

Inches	Cm
¼ inch	0.5 cm
½ inch	1 cm
¾ inch	1.5 cm
1 inch	2.5 cm
2 inches	5 cm
3 inches	7 cm
4 inches	10 cm
5 inches	12 cm
6 inches	15 cm
7 inches	18 cm
8 inches	20 cm
9 inches	23 cm
10 inches	25 cm
11 inches	28 cm
12 inches	30 cm

acknowledgments

I would like to thank the very lovely Kate Whitaker for her beautiful pictures in
this book—she's a girl who really knows how to bring a penguin cupcake to life!

And a huge thank you to Penny Markham for her beautiful plates and
tableware.

To Steve and Céline at Ryland Peters & Small for their patience, utter
fabulousness, and extraordinary hard work.

Also, thank you to our wonderful hand models, Céline, Amy, and Mima for
stepping in and holding piping bags when my hands were covered in frosting
and food coloring!

And to my parents, M and R, an enormous thank you for yet again more dog-
sitting, for just being there when I need you, and for being so wonderful. Mungo
says thanks too!